A SHORT HISTORY OF GERMANY

A SHORT HISTORY
OF GERMANY

by

SIR JOHN K. DUNLOP, K.B.E., C.M.G., M.C., T.D., PH.D.

OSWALD WOLFF

LONDON, W.I

1965

Third Revised and Enlarged
Edition, 1965

MADE AND PRINTED IN GREAT BRITAIN BY
THE GARDEN CITY PRESS LIMITED
LETCHWORTH, HERTFORDSHIRE

CONTENTS

v

TABLE OF MAPS

Page

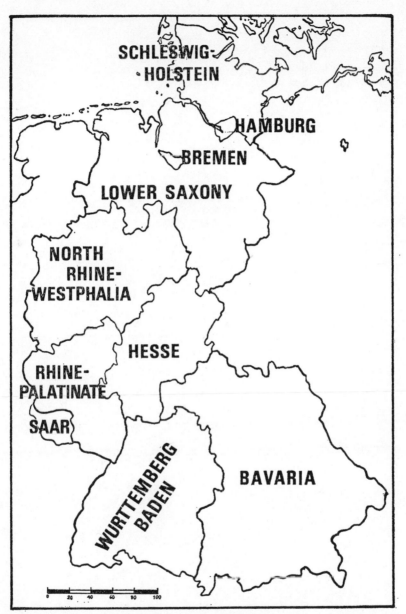

The Federal Republic of Germany 1954.
Showing the boundaries of the Länder and of the British,
French and American Zones.

AUTHOR'S FOREWORD

THE compilation of this book mirrors a score of years in German history. When the war ended in 1945 massive British forces were on German soil as victors, troops of an allied army of occupation. Yet, almost at once, the sheer pressure of surrounding human suffering and need constrained them to turn their skill and energy to the task of mending the ravages of war. I had come from the Allied Military Government and Allied Control Commission in Italy to undertake analogous responsibilities in Germany. It seemed to me to be essential that, so soon as possible, the British troops stationed in Germany should have an opportunity to learn something of the background history of the countryside in which they were living. My diary records that it was as far back as January 10, 1947, that I first gave a talk on Germany and German history to a British battalion then stationed at Buxtehude, near Hamburg. Very many lectures in Germany, and some at Army installations in England, followed that first one. They were issued in note form. Finally, in 1953, the suggestion was made to me that they might form the basis of a book. The proposal received the cordial and invaluable support of the Commander in Chief of the British Army in Germany, General Sir Richard Gale. *A Short History of Germany* in its first form was written in Hamburg in the early summer of 1954. General Gale himself wrote a Foreword. The printing and distribution were undertaken with zeal and efficiency by the Royal Army Ordnance Corps and Royal Army Education Corps. This first edition was published in September 1954. It was written with one particular body of readers in mind, the officers and men of the

British Army of the Rhine and their families. Intentionally it was short. There were only one hundred pages to cover a period which ranged from Julius Caesar to Dr. Adenauer. Because it was written in the British Zone for British troops it did deal more thoroughly with the northern part of modern Germany than with the land as a whole. It was made clear to readers that there would have to be a certain amount of over-simplification. There was a reprint of that first edition which was also produced in Germany. Then, in 1957, a rewritten new edition was produced in England on a commercial basis. This was somewhat longer than the first, but still in the form of a short history, easy to carry and to handle. That issue was soon sold out and it is now not to be obtained in the market. In the meantime history has not stood still. Therefore the decision has been taken to publish, for the third time, *A Short History of Germany*. The text of the second issue has been revised, new pages added and the whole brought up to date. It still is in the form of a short history. The dangers of compression are realized but experience of previous editions seems to confirm the belief that there is a need for a small book which will portray the most important factors which have contributed to the development and history of the land and people of Germany now, as ever, in the centre of Europe.

JOHN K. DUNLOP

Sevenoaks.
April 1964.

CHAPTER ONE

GERMANY IN ROMAN TIMES:
THE BARBARIAN INVASIONS

THE English and the German peoples are closely related one to another in race and in culture. When, in the middle period of the fifth century after Christ, the Angles and Saxons sailed from the coast lands of the Weser and the Elbe or from the Frisian islands to settle in southern and eastern England, there were many of their stock and kindred who remained behind on German soil. Today when school groups or students from the two countries meet it is difficult to identify from outward view, from colour of hair or skin or from the shape of the head, which members of the cheerful company are from southern England and which from northern Germany.

Yet the relationship is that of cousins rather than of brethren. In Great Britain as a whole there exists an important Celtic element which has little equivalent in Germany. Conversely, in Germany east of the river Elbe there is an admixture of Slav blood which has no counterpart in Britain. Nor is there in Britain that southern influence in art, culture and building which so characterizes Bavaria.

During the first fifteen centuries of the Christian era the contacts between England and Germany were slight. True, St. Boniface, Alcuin of York and other missionaries journeyed from England to Germany; Henry the Lion of Saxony and the Emperor Sigismund came to England and there were other, though less notable, visitors. Yet, in general, the traffic between England and Germany in those

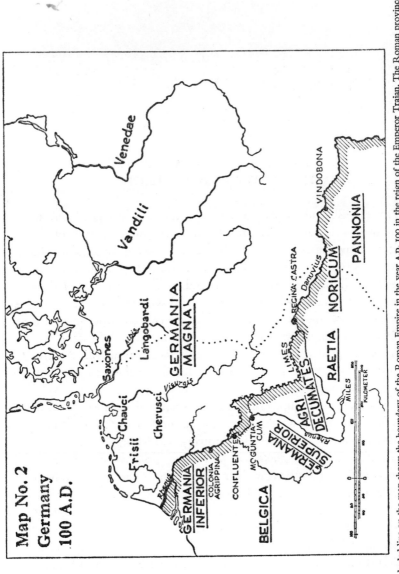

Map No. 2
Germany
100 A.D.

The shaded line on the map shows the boundary of the Roman Empire in the year A.D. 100 in the reign of the Emperor Trajan. The Roman provinces of Germania Inferior, Belgica, Germania Superior, Raetia, Noricum and Pannonia had been established by the death of Augustus A.D. 14. The Agri Decumates were incorporated in the Empire by Domitian A.D. 83 and protected by the fortified 'Limes'. In Germania Magna lived many Germanic tribes, the names of only a few are shown. The Slav peoples lived at this time further east. When, in the fourth and fifth centuries the Germans moved south and west the Slavs moved into the vacant lands, coming as far as the line shown dotted on the map.

centuries was not to be compared with the lively interchange of men and ideas which flowed between the ports of England and her nearest neighbours, France and the Low Countries. Even the Angles and Saxons, once they had settled in England, seem to have retained little contact with the country of their origin. Throughout the Middle Ages the stream of pilgrims, students and merchants went, from England to France, Flanders and Italy. There were those who used the Rhine valley route on their way to Italy, but few seem to have penetrated eastward into Germany. The merchants of the Hanseatic towns had their own house in London at the Steel yard and their agencies at York, Hull and East Anglian ports, but they also kept to the coastal zone.

It was with the beginning of the fifteenth century that there came a change. The Revival of Learning and the Reformation brought to England scholars and divines from the universities of Switzerland, Bohemia and the Netherlands. Later, during the period of the religious wars, Scotsmen, Englishmen, and Irishmen fought for both the Catholic and the Protestant faiths on the plains of Germany. Then, with the arrival of the House of Hanover on the throne of England, there commenced a period of close co-operation between the peoples of Great Britain and Germany, which lasted for two centuries. At first it was chiefly a comradeship in arms. Soldiers from Great Britain fought alongside soldiers from Prussia, Hanover, Brunswick, and Hesse, generally against the French. There was also cultural intercourse, especially in the realms of literature and music. The English Court became closely linked with the princely houses of Germany. Right up to the end of Queen Victoria's reign the German and Austrian watering-places were the favourite resorts of the British aristocracy, and Baedeker's Guides and the Tauchnitz editions of the classics were household words in Victorian middle-class England. With dramatic suddenness this long period of friendship was followed by fifty years of estrangement. Two great wars were fought, bringing much bitterness and distrust into the relations between the two peoples.

Yet there has survived the realization that the fate of the two nations must be closely linked. Today the forces of the two countries exist side by side within the North Atlantic Treaty Organization. Tens of thousands of British soldiers and airmen are stationed in North Germany, and every year sees a lively interchange of tourists and students across the North Sea.

It may well be that the very fact of the close racial and cultural relationship between the English and the German people makes an objective study of German history somewhat difficult for British readers. For the British in so many ways think like the Germans— at all events like the Germans of the north. It has probably been the experience of many of those who arrived in Northern Germany after the end of the war that on first impression it seemed very similar to England. Later came the realization that things were different. Later still, to the wise ones, came the determination to find out how this difference came about.

Certainly the fundamental distinction is geographical. Great Britain is an island, a fortress bounded by a moat. Germany is an expanse of country in the middle of Europe, possessing neither moat nor natural rampart. Neither to the east nor to the west are there arresting physical features to act as an obvious frontier between the German and the Slav, or the German and the Frenchman. In the twenty centuries of the Christian era there have been four special ways in which the story of England and the story of Germany have differed one from another. They could be defined as follows:

Germany as a nation expanded slowly from the Rhine Valley eastward across the Weser, Elbe, and the Oder till it reached the estuary of the Memel.

The Empire of the Middle Ages was regarded as a Universal State, not as a national German institution. Though in practice the Emperor was by race a German, he tended to regard himself as the secular head of Western Christendom, and not as the leader of the German people. Thus "the Imperial

Dream" delayed the formation of a German state around a central kingly family, as happened in England and France. The effect of the Reformation and the Counter-Reformation was destructive of German unity.

National strength developed, not from the centre, but from two frontier states, eventually to be known as Prussia and Austria. Their rivalry delayed German unity.

For the British student of German history it is important to realize at the outset that the Germany of the nineteenth century was in many respects a colonizing Power. It had expanded eastward from the Rhine valley, just as, many years later, the United States and Canada expanded westward from the Atlantic seaboard. So, historically, it lacked that sense of unity given to the English part of Great Britain since the days of Roman administration.

Eighteen hundred years ago, at the end of the first century of the Christian era, nearly all of present-day England lay within the confines of the Roman Empire. That was true of only one part of present-day Germany.

In England civilization and a settled order of life spread northward and westward from the peninsula of Kent and the Home Counties. Roman conquest took the same route. By the first century A.D. a typical Roman culture spread over all the plain lands of the centre and south, so that York, Chester, and Exeter all became small replicas of London, itself a mirror of a Latin city. England, south of Hadrian's Wall, was a settled Roman province. This Roman civilization and administration was to remain for nearly four centuries. When eventually the Roman Empire collapsed and Saxons, Angles, Jutes, and later Danes and Northmen invaded the land there arose a number of tribal kingdoms, seven or more. Yet, chiefly because the land was an island and of manageable size in those days of poor communications, the southern half could be merged into one administrative unit. It had been so organized under the Romans: it was again to be so organized under Duke William the Norman.

5

For nine centuries the boundaries of England have been unchanged on the atlas. Very different indeed is the story of Germany. At the time of writing, when the signing of a Peace Treaty is a remote possibility and when the eastern frontiers of Germany are a matter of high diplomacy, the best course for the objective historian is to point out that over a period of some thousand years the eastern frontier of German influence has moved steadily farther eastward. More recently, in the last half century, as a result of two World Wars that frontier has recoiled considerably to the west. The Germany that our fathers knew, the Germany of Edwardian days, has passed away. Yet it still broods, an uneasy ghost, over Central Europe. This widespread Germany, the empire of Bismarck's creation, will in due time have to be studied. Three definite stages of expansion led to the final form of Bismarck Germany. First there was the "old" Germany of classical times—fundamentally, the land west and south of the Rhine and the Danube. Then there was the "medieval" Germany, stretching out to the frontier marches of Mark Brandenburg and the Ostmark. Finally there was the later Germany, with conquests and extensions far to the east.

The advance and subsequent retreat will have to be studied on a map, for, indeed, a study on the ground is today possible only to a fortunate few. Yet these factors must be understood if there is to be any true appreciation of the problems of today. In the year 1964 the word "Germany," used in conversation or in a newspaper, probably means in fact the Federal Republic of Western Germany. Farther east is the Russian-occupied zone, styled the German Democratic Republic. Farther east still, across the line of the river Oder and the Western Neisse, lie those former German provinces which are today under the Government of Poland, a condition that has not been confirmed by Great Britain in a Peace Treaty. The map will make clear what is interesting and of present-day importance—that a large area of the Federal Republic of today once formed part of the Roman Empire and has a tradition of nearly two thousand years of settled civilization.

In the first century of the Christian era the Roman Empire covered the whole of Western Europe from the Atlantic to the Rhine and the whole of Southern Europe from the Mediterranean to the Danube. To close the angle between the two great rivers the Romans built a line of fortifications, to which they gave the name of the Limes, from a point near Rigomagus (Remagen), which is on the Rhine, to Abusina, upstream of Regina Castra (Regensburg), on the Danube.

The Rhine was a great trade route as well as being a protective moat to the settled lands to the west. On that western—left—bank were the two Roman provinces of Germania Superior (Upper Germany—upper in the sense of being upstream on the Rhine) and Germania Inferior (Lower Germany). On this left bank and in the valley of the Moselle were many Roman cities whose names in recognizable form are with us today. Such were Colonia Agrippinensis (Cologne), Bonna (Bonn), Augusta Trevirorum (Trier), Moguntiacum (Mainz), and so on. In these cities would be found all the normal forms of Roman life—the forum, the baths, the temples, and later the Christian churches.

To the east of the Rhine, save for that frontier province protected by the Limes, there stretched for miles and miles a vast expanse of moor and forest, swamp and sandy plains, called by the Romans Germania Magna (Great Germany). Thus the word "Germany" is among the oldest geographical expressions known to European history. As first used, it referred to an area and not to a special tribe. According to a recent German historian the word may be derived from a Celtic word meaning "neighbour." It has been fixed in history by the monumental work of the Roman writer Tacitus: *De Situ, Moribus et Populis Germanide* ("Concerning the Location, Manners, and Peoples of Germany). The previously quoted German writer adds that the later word deutsch comes from the Old High German diot, meaning "the people." In its adjectival form it was diotisc, and this became latinized into theodiscus and then "teutonic."

Julius Caesar and other Roman writers were very impressed by the vastness of the North German Plain which stretched far beyond their frontier posts. Travellers, it was said, had marched for days on end and had not reached the far boundary of the forests. The historian Gibbon suggests, in an interesting phrase, that the forests and plains of Germania Magna were in climate and character not unlike the interior of Canada in the eighteenth century in which he wrote. From such descriptions as have reached us it seems that Germany was a colder and wetter place than it is today. That is to be expected, for the countryside was still drying out after the last Ice Age. Ten thousand years earlier the massive glaciers of Scandinavian ice had melted and shrunk northward, leaving to the south a ribbed plain of gravel and sand and mud, through which great rivers, unable to find a way south through the Alps, pushed their way along the flank of the ice to the North Sea and the Baltic. Scattered over the plain were heavy boulders of northern granite, carried by the glaciers from the mountains of Norway and Sweden and dropped in North Germany as the ice melted. From the study of the stones geologists can identify their mountain origin in the far north. The casual traveller through the countryside can recognize these great blocks of roughly squared stone, called by the Germans Findlinge, worked into the bottom courses of the brick-built churches of Niedersachsen and Schleswig-Holstein. Before men cleared the forests and drained the swamps the country was certainly much wetter, the rivers wider, than is the case today.

In this tangle of forests, moor, and fen lived the tribes whom Tacitus described as Germans. Perhaps some were a mixture of new arrivals and early aborigines. In general, however, the Germans belonged to the Indo-Germanic stock and they spoke an Aryan language. They came, perhaps, from South Sweden or from the Southern Baltic. In Germany they were hunters, fishers, the keepers of small herds of cattle, and the cultivators of small fields near their tribal settlements. As yet they had no towns worthy of the name; there were only family or tribal villages. Because in the land of their wanderings there was little stone and few caves, they built their

8

primitive huts of poles and thatch and mud, easy to build and probably readily abandoned when crop exhaustion or enemy pressure urged a tribal move.

In front of the Roman defensive line formed by the Rhine, the Limes, and the Danube there stretched a zone of Latin influence which reached the Weser and in the north as far as the Elbe. Hereabouts there were trading stations of Romans or, more likely, Romanized Celts. There was a Roman track which ran along the south bank of the Lippe from the Rhine almost as far as Paderborn. We know that the settlement at Stade, near the Elbe estuary, had a population which was acquainted with Roman culture, for domestic pottery excavated on that site shows Roman shape and design. Chieftains from these parts would visit the Roman civilization west of the Rhine; some even visited Rome, and certainly many took service in the Roman army. Tacitus says that the Germans had no written language. It is to be guessed that some of those who traded local products for Roman manufactures would learn to speak and possibly even to write Latin.

One of the few pieces of early German history that may come the way of the English schoolboy is the story of Varus and his Legions. The Roman general Varus, marching into North Germany in A.D. 9 with three Roman legions, the seventeenth, eighteenth, and nineteenth, and supporting cavalry, reached and fortified himself in camp at Minden. The strength of a legion was just over six thousand men. Auxiliary troops would perhaps bring the total forces to thirty thousand. Hermann, or, in Latin, Arminius, the chief of the Cheruski, a local German clan, himself trained to war in Roman service, rallied the tribes around him. The Romans broke camp and marched to destruction. The site of the battle is a matter for academic dispute. The monument to commemorate the victory is on the hills overlooking Detmold. Modern historians are more inclined to place the battle near Osnabruck on the Vennermoor.

Romantic and patriotic German historians have made Hermann one of the great heroes of all time. It is a sober historical fact that within a few years other Roman generals and other armies marched through Germany over the battlefield of Varus' defeat and rescued trophies lost in the disaster. Nevertheless, the psychological shock of the defeat was great. So was the military effect, for the total garrison along the length of the Rhine was only five legions. If the prize had seemed worth while Rome might have persevered with the conquest of Germany. But the country was vast and uninviting, the people warlike and evasive.

Therefore the legions held the Rhine and the Germans remained in the forests and the moorland. Gibbon had a pleasant phrase: "The irregular divisions and restless motions of the people of Germany dazzle our imagination and seem to multiply their numbers." In fact, however, it seems likely that their numbers were indeed increasing rapidly. Tradition describes them as a fecund race. Tacitus thought that the men were lazy. In our own country, one of their tribes, the Saxons, were to prove themselves masterly foresters. With their iron axes they felled the primeval English forests to clear space for their fields in a way the Celts and Romans had never done. So perhaps they were also clearing the German forests and increasing their settlements.

The great North European Plain which stretches from the shores of Holland to the Ural Mountains was in the first centuries of our Christian era a trackless expanse. Such clearings as man had made were but a minute acreage among a waste of forest and moor. Yet, though trackless, it was by no means impassable. No mountain range, arid table-land, or sandy desert imposed a physical barrier to movement. Tribes willing to move slowly, on foot, accompanied by their flocks and simple household goods, could travel without real difficulty, south and east, as their supply of food decided or fear impelled. There were as yet no cities, holy places, or specially favoured localities which might have fixed men in permanent settlements. The mass of humanity from the Rhine to the Volga was politically shapeless and instable.

That great migration, which the German historians call the

Volkerwanderung and the British, less politely, the Barbarian Invasion, was no sudden wave, no dramatic bursting of the frontier walls. Probably, outside the vision of Roman historians, the German people had been moving westward or southward for many years. About the fourth century the Goths, cousins to Tacitus' Germans, coming out of the plains of Poland, moved south and then west through Hungary and Italy and eventually to France and Spain. The Vandals moving out of Prussia descended on North Italy, the Burgundians into the territory which still bears their name. The tribes nearest the old Roman frontier made the shortest moves. The Allemanni from Southern Germany crossed the Rhine and established themselves in Eastern France. From their tribal name comes the word "Allemagne," used today in French to denote the whole of Germany. One separate segment of this "wandering of the peoples" carried the kindred tribes of Saxons, Angles, and Jutes from the country around the Elbe estuary and from the western shores of Denmark to the British Isles. While most of this Germanic migration was slow—a move of families with flocks and herds, there was another, non-German, irruption which was more violent and spectacular. In the middle of the fifth century the Huns, a Mongolian folk, came on horseback as raiders under their dreaded chieftain Attila. They rode over the Hungarian plains and penetrated deep into France before they were eventually checked at the battle of Troyes.

As the Germans moved south and west, leaving the river basins of the Vistula and the Oder, so Slav tribes came behind them into the vacant land. When eventually the Germanic movement came to a halt the forward line of Slav settlement had reached Lower Holstein, the middle Elbe, Thuringia, and Bohemia. The line on the map (p.18) which marks the westward limit of Slav settlements more than a thousand years ago is dramatically close to that other line which represents on the maps of today the Iron Curtain between west and east.

By about A.D. 600 the main easterly move of German and

Slav peoples had come to an end. The Angles, Saxons, and Jutes were in England, the Franks, Burgundians, and Allemanni were in Gaul, Lombards and Venetians were in Italy, Goths in Spain. East of the Rhine, between the old Roman frontiers and the Slavs, lived the Saxons, Swabians, Frisians, and Bavarians.

The Angles and Saxons, heathens when they reached England, exterminated the Celtic Christians and slew the monks. But in the end they were themselves converted to the Christian faith by the Celtic missionaries from Ireland and Southern Scotland and by the mission from Rome led by St. Augustine. In Gaul and in Italy the Germanic invaders accepted the Christian faith and the traditions of Roman culture which they found in the cities and countryside. But east of the Rhine the Saxons and the other tribes were heathen.

The years between A.D. 600 and A.D. 700 may therefore be regarded as the still water between tides: the westward move of the Germanic tribes was coming to an end. Henceforward the German peoples were to commence a long continued march towards the east, back across the lands from which their ancestors had migrated. This move was to owe its strength to the Frankish tribes and to Christian missionaries, many of these were monks from England.

The Franks had established themselves in the fertile lands which lie athwart the Lower Rhine and the Moselle, with the tribal centre of gravity at Aachen. From this race there was to come a succession of three generations of leaders, Charles the Hammer (Charles Martel), Pepin the Short, and Charles the Great (Charlemagne, Karl der Grosse). It was in the reign of Charles Martel that Boniface, an English monk, commenced his missionary journeys to the Saxons. He established a monastery at Fulda, on the Upper Weser, in the heart of heathen Saxony, and from this centre Christian teaching radiated among the Germans. He was slain while preaching to the Frisians in A.D. 755. Without doubt his work prepared the way for the even greater developments in the time of Charlemagne.

Charlemagne—Carolus Magnus of the Latin texts—was, by any standard, one of the great figures of German and of West European history. From his palace at Aachen his influence and his activities radiated in every direction: into France, into Italy, and, which concerns this record, into Germany. For with Charlemagne the eastward trek began. He was to carry his Frankish rule, his Christian bishops, and his Celtic-Roman scholarship into the midst of a kindred German people, the Saxons of the North German Plain. The impetus of Charlemagne's easterly move from out of the Rhine Valley was to endure for centuries.

In three decisive campaigns Charlemagne marched his armies to the Elbe and the Danube. Local legend says that in A.D. 797 he rode his horse to the top of a sand dune near Cuxhaven and looked away over the seas to the north. Wherever he went he took with him Christian bishops and teachers; many of these were English, trained in the school of the Venerable Bede. Alcuin of York, Charlemagne's greatest friend and adviser, was such a one. Another was Wilhardus, a Northumbrian, who was the first Bishop of Bremen. Students of history are warned that violent changes are seldom enduring, Charlemagne produced the exception. In a few short years he changed the picture of the North German Plain. Where previously there had been the rude settlements of heathen savages there were now Christian bishoprics. Within a short space of time Charlemagne established bishops at Münster, Osnabruck, Paderborn, Minden, Bremen, Verden, Hildesheim, and Halberstadt. Tradition ascribes the settlement at Hamburg to Charlemagne. Certainly a bishopric and a fort, the Hammaburg, were founded there by his son Lewis the Pious.

Contemplating the great success of his achievement, one may reflect that Charlemagne did enjoy three advantages denied to most of those who came after him. First, and perhaps as important as all else, he possessed a strong frame and a splendid constitution. Thanks to his physical fitness he ruled for fifty years. That was a very unusual span of life in days when the human body was beset by the dangers of unhealthy living and incurable disease. Secondly, he was able to operate from the firm base of a fertile and prosperous family inheritance in his own land of the Franks. Finally, and allied to the last-named advantage, he possessed, in his capital city of Aachen, a centre well situated and secure from raiding attacks.

On Christmas Day A.D. 800, while on a visit to Rome, Charlemagne was crowned with the Imperial Crown and was thus proclaimed the successor to the Roman Emperor. It is said by some historians that he was surprised and displeased at this papal act. Regarded in the light of history, the attempt to use the personal brilliancy of a great Frankish king to reassert the glory of the Western Empire was either too early or too late. Charlemagne himself had only fourteen more years of life. His tremendous energy and ability had kept his realm together. When he died two completely contradictory forces strove for mastery. The Church wished to maintain the power of the Emperor and, for that purpose, to apply the law of primogeniture, the inheritance of the title and estate by the eldest son, to the exclusion, or at least relative exclusion, of all other sons. It was the Frankish tradition, however, that family property should be divided among all sons, and, from the point of view of Charlemagne's own family, his kingdom was as divisible as if it had been a family landed estate. It may here be mentioned that this same Frankish tradition has continued to leave its mark on German history as well as on German social customs. In parts of Germany, notably in Hesse, minute farms have been divided into still more minute fragments in order that all sons might have a share. Throughout the Middle Ages and late into the eighteenth century dukedoms and principalities were perpetually being broken up by death and reunited in different manner by marriage, just as if the land and its inhabitants were the personal chattels of the reigning prince. Even today in Germany all sons and daughters take the father's title of nobility, so that Graf and Grafin, Baron and Baronesse, are much more frequent currency in the drawing-rooms of Germany than are grades of nobility in Great Britain.

For a few short years after the death of Charles the Great his son

Lewis of Aquitaine, the Pious (Ludwig der Fromme), reigned alone, if such a phrase can be used to describe a life ceaselessly troubled by strife with his own sons. At his death the Frankish tradition triumphed. In A.D. 843, at the town of Verdun, the three sons of Lewis signed a treaty which is one of the memorable documents of European history. The great empire was divided into three pieces. The territory of the west Franks went to Charles the Bald; at a later date men would call that land France. The territory of the east Franks went to Lewis the German (Ludwig der Deutsche). The eldest son, Lothar, gained the imperial title and with it a narrow strip of country which started in the north of Belgium, ran through Lotharingia, which we today call Lorraine, through Burgundy, and on into Italy. It was a kingdom clumsy to administer and impossible to defend. In fact the problem was not put to the test, for Lothar died without heirs. There was a second treaty, almost as important as the first, signed at Meersen in A.D. 870. The middle kingdom of Lothar was divided between the other two brothers. Alsace, Lorraine, and most of Burgundy went to the east Franks—that is to say, to the German branch. Thereafter east Franks and west Fanks went forward each in their own way.

Since Lewis the Pious, son of Charles the Great, only two men have ruled over the combined lands of France and Germany, each for a short time and each by force of arms and not *de jure*. They were Napoleon Bonaparte and Adolf Hitler.

CHAPTER TWO

MEDIEVAL GERMANY AND THE IMPERIAL DREAM
(900–1500)

WHEN Duke William the Norman defeated Harold of England at the battle of Hastings in the year 1066 he won the crown of England. True, it took him sixteen more years to complete his conquest and to beat down local revolts. Yet by the year 1085, less, therefore, than a score of years after his crossing of the Channel, he was in a position to order the compilation of Domesday Book. This great statistical record of the state of the countryside, its tenancy system, and its agricultural capacity was carried out by commissioners sent in the King's name to every shire in the land.

There are few single items which reflect in so striking a measure the difference between the history of England and that of Germany. The administrative success of the Domesday Book in England emphasises the realization that such a proceeding would have been quite impossible in Germany, not only in the year 1085, but for nearly eight centuries thereafter.

England and, at later dates, France, Scotland, and Sweden were able to coalesce round a central kingly house. That solution was to fail in Germany. Partly the failure was due to the lack of a fixed geographical boundary. Partly it was certainly due to the great area covered by the German tribes. Yet perhaps the strongest element working against the centralized monarchy was the tradition of the Holy Roman Empire—the Imperial Dream. How this idea reflected itself in German history must now be studied, for the results of that Imperial Dream are with the world today.

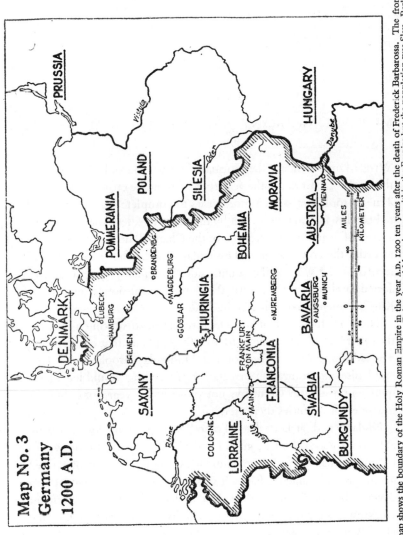

Map No. 3
Germany
1200 A.D.

The map shows the boundary of the Holy Roman Empire in the year A.D. 1200 ten years after the death of Frederick Barbarossa. The frontier to the east was still fluid. Pommerania was still ruled by Slav princes. Bohemia and Moravia were within the Empire but the population was Slav. Berlin had not yet become a city. The Teutonic knights had not yet landed in Prussia. The first Cistercian monastery had been settled on the Oder in Silesia.

When the great and personal empire of Charlemagne was divided among his sons those of the German tribes who lived in the Rhine Valley and the lands east of it went their own way. Although for a time nominally united under the heirs of Lewis the German, the great tribal groups of Saxons, Swabians, Bavarians, Burgundians, and the east Franks (later usually called Franks or Frankonians) behaved much like the great clans of Scotland. They were prepared to acknowledge a nominal king only on condition that he did not interfere with their own internal affairs.

While Western Christendom was without one strong directing hand her enemies were crowding in on every side. The northern coasts were harried by Northmen and Danes; Moslem power was firmly entrenched in Spain and was raiding the southern shores of Italy. Then, across the plains of Europe, appeared a new threat in the onward move of the Magyars, or, as they are usually called by historians, the Hungarians. It was this last danger which caused the German clans to rally for a time under one chieftain, Henry the Fowler (Heinrich der Volger), leader of the Saxons. In a battle on the river Unstrut in A.D. 933 he defeated the Magyar hordes. Such was the prestige gained by this victory that Henry was able to secure from the other tribes their consent to the succession, on his death, by his son Otto. The kingship was in no sense hereditary. It was only the instinct of self-preservation against the threat from without which made the other German tribes realize the wisdom of continuing the leadership in the hands of a strong Duke of Saxony. Otto, crowned King of the Germans at Aachen, justified his election by a second and decisive victory over the Magyars on the Lechfeld, in Bavaria, in A.D. 955. Though the coronation at Aachen had made him King of the Germans it had not made him Emperor. This could be achieved only by a coronation at Rome. Otto wanted the imperial title, and it suited Pope John XII to gain the protection of this powerful German against threats from local princes in Lombardy. So, on February 2, 962, Otto of Saxony was crowned Emperor in Rome. From now on, for some four centuries,

German princes, surnamed emperors, were to be inextricably entangled in Italian politics.

Certainly, the lure of the south was partly due to the attractions of a sunny climate and a cultured manner of life. Partly it was due to the religious link with Rome. There was also the pull of the century-old trading routes and of the well-worn pilgrim way to Italy. The road to the south from the Rhine Valley over the St. Gotthard, or the more easterly route by the Main Valley across the Danube and over the Brenner—these were ways known to the Romans. Along these roads lay great cities and staging posts ready for the overnight guest.

North Germany was a trackless waste. As late as the fifteenth century a merchant of Frankfurt-on-Main or of Augsburg would regard a journey to Milan or Venice as far less tiring and taking far less time than a journey to Brunswick or Magdeburg.

Moreover, the link with Italy accorded with the medieval conception of the Empire and the Papacy. The Nation, as we understand it today, as it was to be conceived in England as early as the fourteenth century and in France somewhat later, had little meaning to medieval man. He had loyalty to his clan or to his city. Beyond that there was the great sense of membership of one universal Christian Church. Because that Church was a body political as well as a body spiritual, it was thought proper that there should be two heads; a spiritual head—the Pope—and a Secular head—the Emperor. The medieval mind expressed this idea in the metaphor of the two swords which defended the Christian faith, the sword of the spirit, wielded by the Pope, and the sword of military power, wielded by the Emperor. In fact, this medieval conception of the Emperor was never given any real chance of success, because in the important central period of the Middle Ages the selection of the man who should be the head of Western Christendom became involved in the mutual rivalry of the German tribes. This destroyed the possibility of continuous administration. It would appear fantastic to present ideas of government that the

Emperor Frederick Barbarossa (Friedrich Rotbart) had, in practice, no fixed capital. The centre of the empire was where the emperor happened to be at the time—whether in Germany, in North Italy, or on the march to the crusades. That a German prince should go campaigning against Saracens in South Italy to the neglect of his homeland would seem contrary to our modern thought. But to Frederick Barbarossa, as to Richard the Lionheart of England, logistical considerations or arguments of statecraft had no valid place when the challenge of the Christian faith called to a crusade. It was work which was laid in their hands, and they must do it.

The history of those four centuries was also decisively affected by two other disputes: the struggle between the Emperor and the Papacy, and the struggle between the house of Hohenstaufen (also called the Waiblings or the Ghibellines) and the Saxon house of Welf or Guelf, as it was called in Italy.

Otto I, to strengthen his own hold over the country and as a balance against the tribal dukedoms of Burgundy, Swabia, and Frankonia, increased the powers of the bishops. In particular, those bishoprics established in North Germany by Charlemagne and by Lewis the Pious received rich gifts of land from the Saxon Emperor. As a result, a large part of the Saxon and Westphalian lands, which nine centuries later were to be called the British Zone of Germany, became from the eleventh century onward the domain of powerful prince-bishops. Such were the bishoprics of Münster, Bremen, Verden, Paderborn, and Hildesheim. So also was the older and traditional archbishopric of Cologne. What Otto and his successors wanted were sound, loyal, and efficient clerical vice-regents. The spiritual value of their way of life did not greatly concern the Emperors, and if the bishops chose to marry that did not seem to the Emperor to be a question of great moment. To the Papal Chair at Rome, however, came a line of reforming Popes inspired by the zeal of the Cluniac monasteries. What Pope Gregory VII (Hildebrand) wished was that the bishops should be pious churchmen, not necessarily German, but the best men available, devoted in their loyalty to their spiritual lord at Rome. These two contesting lines of thought led to the great "Investiture" stuggle. The question was: Who should appoint these powerful and important German bishops? Although a German Emperor had to humiliate himself before the Pope at Canossa in 1077, in the end victory lay with the German contention. The German bishops continued to be Germans, the strongest supporters of the German Emperor.

Otto I and his successors, Otto II and Otto III, were from the house of Welf. The family originally came from Bavaria, but acquired by marriage the position of leadership over the virile Saxon clans who lived on the North German Plain where now lie Hanover and Oldenburg.

There were four Emperors of this Saxon family. To them is due the credit for that vital move in German history when they led their Saxons across the Elbe and began to colonize the border marches which the Germans called Mark Brandenburg, Ukermark, and so on.

It was the last of the Saxon Emperors, Henry II, who first built the "Kaiserhaus" at Goslar. This long, grey stone building is the oldest secular building now standing in Germany. It was meant to be the meeting-place of the Emperor's Council, the first conception of a settled physical centre for the Empire. A later Emperor, Henry III, the Salian, enlarged it, but it was wrecked in later wars and fell into disrepair and ruins. Its modern form owes its decoration to the romantic ideas of nineteenth-century restorers. However, it is in the little town of Goslar and particularly, in the Kaiserhaus that the British visitor may perhaps catch a vision of "the Imperial Dream."

Following the Saxon line came four Emperors from the Frankish country south of the Moselle. Their family burial place was the cathedral at Speyer, and, so far as they could be said to have had a capital city, it was that town. When this line failed the Saxons might reasonably have hoped for the Imperial crown. Instead it when to the Hohenstaufens, princes from Swabia, whose family name came from the small city of Waiblingen, near Stuttgart.

Nearly every British visitor to Germany will some time or other during his stay hear the name of Friedrich Barbarossa of the House of Hohenstaufen. The very style, with its German Christian name and Italian nickname, tells the story of the man, Frederick of the Red Beard, or Kaiser Rotbart, as he may be called in various stories. Friedrich Barbarossa and Charlemagne are the two great figures of early and medieval German history. Barbarossa succeeded his uncle in 1152 and reigned for thirty-eight years over Germany until, at the age of sixty-five, leading a crusading army through Asia Minor on its march to the Holy Land, he died of a chill caught when bathing in the over-cold waters of the stream Saleph. In his death as in his life he was the typical figure of romantic German chivalry. His life was spent in almost constant warfare and ever on the move. Within five years of his accession to the throne Friedrich had led his army across the Oder into what was then Poland, not on a career of territorial conquest, but to place his own candidate, Duke Wladislaw, on the throne of Poland. Friedrich's reign was dominated by two great struggles and by one diplomatic success. His success was the marriage of his son Henry to Constanze, the heiress to the wealthy and prosperous kingdom of Sicily, which in those days extended into much of Southern Italy. His struggles were, firstly, to expand and secure the Imperial power in Italy and secondly, to win in Germany the age-long battle between the Hohenstaufens and the Welfs. In Italy he had to endure many disappointments. In 1176 at the battle of Legnano his army was thoroughly defeated by the citizens of Milan. He failed to subdue the Swiss, and his army was smitten by pestilence before the gates of Rome.

His fight against the Welfs, and particularly against their great leader, Duke Henry the Lion, was more successful, partly because Henry's own conduct caused discontent among his subjects. Victory came to Barbarossa only after many years of struggle, but the end was decisive. The great Dukedom, stretching from the North Sea to the Alps, was broken up. Bavaria, the original home of the Welfs, was given to Otto of Wittelsbach, and henceforward this

23

principality went its own individualistic way. Only Brunswick and Lüneburg remained Welfish possessions. The new lands of Saxony, those astride the Elbe and down as far as the Bohemian frontier, were given to the family of Wettin, supporters of the Hohenstaufens. With the new lands went the title of the Duke of Saxony. So comes about the confusing historical nomenclature which fixed the kingdom of Saxony with its capital city at Dresden and a principality of Sachsen-Anhalt with its capital at Magdeburg, both far away from the original home of the great Saxon tribe. It was left to the British Military Government to create, in 1946, in the modern Land Niedersachsen, a territory which corresponds fairly closely to the original domain of Henry the Lion. Barbarossa's son, Henry VI, might have been an even greater Emperor than his father, but he died after a reign of only six years. After him came Emperors from outside the Hohenstaufen house, and then, in A.D. 1212, the last and intellectually most brilliant of the line, Friedrich II. Son of a German father and a Sicilian mother, Friedrich loved his South Italian home. Round his court were gathered some of the most brilliant men of intellect of his day. He himself was a scholar and philosopher. He saw himself the Emperor of a great West European civilization which should include not only his cold, dull German subjects, but also his more sparkling Sicilians, his Milanese, and his Romance-speaking Burgundians. Yet, in fact, constant quarrels with the Pope and constant conflicts in Germany made harsh reality very different from his splendid aspirations. The Holy Roman Empire, it has been said, was the "embodiment of that aspiration for order and harmony which the reason of man is always pleased to entertain and his perversity is surely to frustrate." After Friedrich's death there was a brief and sad epilogue. His son Konrad and his grandson Konradin continued to fight to maintain the position in Italy. But at the battle of Tagliacozzo, in Italy, Konradin fell into the hands of Charles of Anjou and was beheaded. So ended the male line of the Hohenstaufens.

There is a German legend of the great King who sleeps in a

cavern in the Kyffhäuser hills, so old that his beard has grown through the table before his chair. Some day, when the ravens no longer fly round the hills, he will awake, take up his spear and shield, and save his people from their enemies. That legend was first told of Frederick II of Sicily. It was the later romanticists who transferred the story to Friedrich Barbarossa.

Precisely because the central power had wandered off into Italy, and because rivalry between Welf and Waibling had led each of them to seek allies in the other camp, the great tribal dukedoms in Germany had split into smaller units. In particular the Emperor, using one of those powers which no man denied him, had granted charters of self-government to many cities. Monasteries had spread from the mother houses in France or the Rhineland right across Germany, and these monasteries had acquired local prestige, position, and power. It was, as it were, a by-product of the failure of the Imperial Dream that Germany of the Middle Ages was very particularly a Germany of cities and monasteries. While princes squandered their substance in mutual wars the cities were prospering. One of the great trade-routes of the Middle Ages brought Eastern spices and Eastern ware by water to Venice, over the Brenner Pass to South Germany, and then across country to cities such as Augsburg, Frankfurt, and Cologne.

As in Roman times, the Rhine was one of the great trade routes of the day. It is interesting to note that Chaucer in his *Canterbury Tales* says of the Wife of Bath that she made a pilgrimage to Cologne, almost the only mention of a German city in *The Canterbury Tales*. The Rhine Valley of today, with its cathedrals, its free cities, its universities, and its ruined baronial castles on the rocky peaks, is a picture frame for those who can mentally reconstruct the outline of the bustling, vivid Germany of the Middle Ages.

The silver mines in the Harz Mountains, near Goslar, had been known in the tenth century. One of the important factors in the struggle between the Welfs and the Waiblings was the contest for the possession of these important mines. In the course of the next three or four hundred years silver and lead mines were discovered and worked in the Tyrol, in Bohemia, and in Hungary. Mining became a recognized industry, and the trade in metals brought wealth to the cities. Great banking houses, at their head the Fuggers of Augsburg, were acquiring riches and power far greater than those of the impoverished barons of the countryside. The master craftsmen and the merchants of these medieval German cities were men of strong character and fierce independence. There was, indeed, a great deal of self-government in democratic form. The Hansa towns—Lübeck, Hamburg, Stade, Bremen, and the like—governed themselves by a council, *ein ehrbarer Rat*, elected from among the wealthier citizens. In the countryside the more important farmers gathered together two or three times a year to organize their local government. It is a tradition that in the moorland south of Cuxhaven this meeting used to take place in a certain meadow, on horseback—surely an excellent way of ensuring that speechmaking should not be too long.

These medieval cities fought hard for self-government. Bremen made life so uncomfortable for the Bishop that he fixed the headquarters of his see at the small village of Bremervorde. Hamburg never accepted the vague overlordship of the Dukes of Lauenburg. Already in the fifteenth century can be noted a characteristic which has lasted to the present day, that German institutions are immature and slow to develop at the higher levels, but that organization is efficient in smaller units such as the city or the corporation or their modern equivalent, the factory.

It was in the cities that medieval life was at its most brilliant and most productive. Hard work, technical ability, and pride of craft flourished in Nuremberg, Augsburg, Frankfurt-on-Main, Goslar, Cologne, and many other cities. There men built Gothic cathedrals and town halls, carved wood and stone, and wrought in iron and bronze. By their engravings and paintings they made the name of German craftsmanship famous in the West. It was in Mainz in 1447 that Johann Gensfleisch zum Gutenberg first printed a book from movable metal types. Perhaps the credit for this epoch-making discovery should be shared with the Dutchman Laurenz Coster—but at all events it was in the German cities that the invention spread with speed. Before long there were presses in Strasburg, Cologne, Bamberg, Nuremberg, and Augsburg, all of them, be it noted, Free Cities of the Empire, not controlled by bishops or local barons. For many decades Germans were the printers for Europe.

The fact that this busy life of craft and letters was based on the cities rather than on a royal court was going to lead to interesting developments. Early German poetry, the first forms of the *Nibelungenlied* and other epics, had developed with the Minnesanger—the court minstrels. Now, however, the focus of poetry and writing was to move to the towns. A Cambridge professor, Herford, who wrote in the middle of the last century, uses a striking phrase: "To a degree unparalleled elsewhere in Europe, literature became plebeian." He follows it up with an interesting description.

> "It was a literature of the workshop and the stall, a literature of men habitually familiar to brutality, plain spoken to grossness, drastic in their ridicule, ferocious in their earnestness, not without sterling honesty but wanting in the grace of good manners, in chivalry, in subtle and delicate intellect."

Today German humour, especially political satire, appears to the British mind to be coarse and crude. Perhaps, after all, it is a direct descendant of the townsman's jesting in the medieval cities. Shakespeare drew plenty of material from the rough humour of Southwark streets, but he was also under the powerful influence of the cultured court of a virgin Queen who, on her own testimony, knew six languages besides her own.

Two other main factors must be mentioned before closing the chapter on medieval Germany. Not through any definite Imperial policy, but as a result of the energies of local barons, of adventurers, and, above all, of the monastic orders, German civilization between the tenth and fourteenth centuries was pressing steadily

27

eastward. Particularly on the upper waters of the Oder, in the land later to be called Silesia, Cisterician monasteries were establishing themselves in the centre of a sparse and primitive Slav population. From these monasteries radiated German culture, improved agriculture, rudimentary knowledge of medicine, and the conception of a settled life.

This eastward move of settlers across the Elbe and later across the Oder resembles in many ways the much later westward movement of colonists in North America. The immense migration was not the result of some act of imperial statecraft, but it was the result of the combined wills of a number of small units inspired by a common idea. Into the sparsely peopled Slav lands came the stalwart peasant families from Westphalia or Friesland, bringing their heavy ploughs, their improved methods of farming, clearing the forests and draining the marshes. Their village settlements were usually built in one straight line along a street, a design markedly different from the circular village plan of the Slav. Prominent among the farmhouses stood the larger house of the Junker, often enough the founder of the settlement. Near by were the church and vicarage, soon to be accompanied by the school.

A recent writer has suggested that the story of the Pied Piper of Hamelin has its origin in the memories of some such migration. He suggests that the sad day when a great number of young men and maidens, not children, left the small town in the wake of an enthusiastic colonizer became so fixed in local tradition that legends grew up around it. Whether this explanation be true or not, it does serve to dramatize the effect which this large-scale emigration must have had on many a town and village in Saxony and Westphalia.

Farther north, along the shores of the Baltic, communities of German traders were moving by sea route faster and farther afield than the farming settlers travelling on foot or by wagon. Before long there were German trading stations at Rostock, Stralsund, Danzig; then Memel, Riga, and Reval. As the Baltic coastlands opened up there was trade in timber, furs, and pitch from these new territories in exchange for woollen goods from England and the Netherlands, Eastern spices from the markets of the Rhineland, and red wine from France. To facilitate commerce, to keep open the seas against pirates or the restraint of princes, these cities and many others banded themselves together in a "Hanse," a league of merchant towns.

Thus, as in the heartland of medieval Germany, so in the frontier marches and the Baltic harbours, it was hard work, craftsmanship, and family loyalty which were making Germany prosperous—and not policy or statecraft, which were, indeed, strikingly absent.

One historical document of first importance was soon to show the meaning of this eastward move. Charles IV, Emperor of Germany, son of that blind King John of Bohemia, as every English schoolboy knows, fell fighting at the battle of Crecy, desired to regularize the manner of election of the Emperor. In the year 1356 he produced his new regulations in the form of the "Golden Bull." Henceforward, it was laid down, there should be seven Electors to choose the Emperor, four of these to be secular princes and three to be princes of the Church. The laymen were the Palgrave of the Rhine, the Duke of Sachs-Wittenberg, whose territory lay on the middle Elbe, the Markgraf of Brandenburg, and the King of Bohemia. The three clerics were the Archbishops of Treves, Cologne, and Mainz. The succession to the lay electorates was by the law of primogeniture. Lord Bryce has said of the Golden Bull that it "legalized anarchy and called it a constitution." On the other hand it is difficult to see what better solution might have been achieved in the temper of the times. Four of the great historical families of Germany were represented in the four lay Electors: the Wittelsbachs of the Palatinate, the Wettins in Sachs-Wittenberg, the Habsburgs in Bohemia, and, within a few years, a Hohenzollern would come to Berlin. One traditional family remained outside the sacred circle. Three centuries must elapse before a Welf of Hanover obtained the electoral hat.

This chapter commenced with the election of an emperor by the great clans of the Saxons, the Bavarians, the Franks, the Swabians, and the Burgundians. The terms of the Golden Bull show how power has shifted to the east and towards the Church. Brandenburg, Sachs-Wittenberg, and Bohemia were barely thought of in A.D. 900.

As the Middle Ages came to an end two further dynastic moves of importance took place. The Emperor Sigismund, successor to Charles IV, and, incidentally, one of the few medieval Emperors who ever visited London, became by marriage heir to the Mark Brandenburg. Content with his own hereditary dominions, he gave his title and the territory of Brandenburg to a personal supporter, Friedrich of Nuremberg, of the House of Hohenzollern.

Already the House of Habsburg had been established in the border duchy of Ostmark, soon to be known as Austria. In the year 1438 Albert of Habsburg was elected the Holy Roman Emperor. From his election to the abolition of the Holy Roman Empire at the behest of Napoleon in 1806 every Emperor came from the House of Habsburg, save when Francis of Lorraine held the Emperor's title as husband of Maria Theresa, heiress of the Habsburg line.

Thus, as the Middle Ages closed, the two great houses, Hohenzollern and Habsburg, were established in their respective capitals of Berlin and Vienna. From these two cities, north and south, they would in the future greatly influence the destiny of Germany, sometimes in partnership, but all too often in rivalry.

CHAPTER THREE

THE REFORMATION AND THE WARS OF RELIGION
(1500–1648)

IN the Middle Ages pious men had dreamed of a splendid Christian State on earth, united in faith and brotherly love, a spiritual and temporal whole, defended against the heathen by the strong sword of the Emperor, nurtured and guided in faith by the wisdom and knowledge of the Pope. By the end of the fifteenth century there was little left of the splendour of that dream . . . National kings were in conflict with the Emperor. For seventy years, from 1306 to 1376, the Pope had been an exile at Avignon, in the south of France, a virtual prisoner of French policy. Worse still had followed: the Emperor and the King of France had openly championed rival candidates for the Papal throne. The Great Schism had shown to the scandalized world Pope and Antipope fulminating one against the other. When at last the Papacy returned to Rome in the early days of the fifteenth century there followed a succession of Popes from the Roman nobility, all more concerned with the extension and safeguarding of the Papal territories in Italy than with the clamant need for a spiritual revival within the Church.

For there was ferment abroad. Learning, stimulated by the discovery of printing, was spreading through the towns and universities. Lawyers, merchants, professors, the wealthy burghers of the new middle classes, were now able to read—indeed, to form small libraries of their own. Sometimes the books they purchased were in Greek or Latin, either classics from the golden days of Athens and

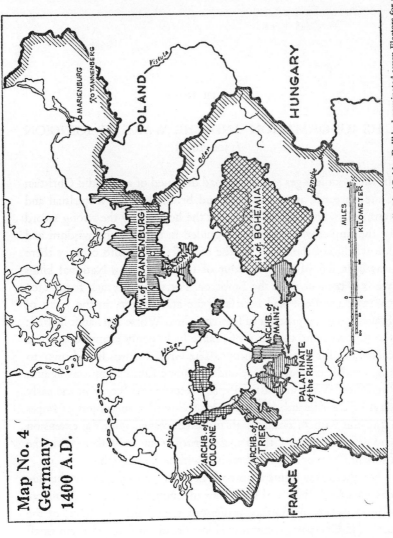

Map No. 4
Germany
1400 A.D.

MARIENBURG
TANNENBERG
POLAND
Vistula
Oder
W. of BRANDENBURG
SAXONY
Elbe
Weser
K. of BOHEMIA
Danube
ARCHB. of MAINZ
PALATINATE of the RHINE
HUNGARY
ARCHB. of COLOGNE
ARCHB. of TRIER
Rhine
FRANCE

MILES
KILOMETER

The map shows the boundary of the Holy Roman Empire in A.D. 1400. Forty years earlier the 'Golden Bull' had nominated seven Electors for the Empire. The map shows their territories. In 1400 the Teutonic Knights controlled the land, then called Pomerellia, astride the lower waters of the Vistula. Ten years later in A.D. 1410 at the battle of Tannenberg the Knights were defeated by Poland and Pomerellia became Polish thus dividing Prussia from Brandenburg.

Rome or works written by scholars of the Middle Ages. In ever-increasing measure, however, writers and printers produced books in the language of their own country, sometimes translations of classical works, sometimes original writings of new authors.

In Germany especially men were reading the philosophical writings of classical times, and they were reading the early fathers of the Christian faith. Much of what they read seemed superior in thought and piety to the actual practice of bishops, priests, and monks in the Church they saw around them. For the Catholic Church, as it emerged from the Middle Ages, was wealthy and somnolent. Two Councils, at Constance and Basle, had failed to produce reforms. Not all its servants were men of exemplary life. Chaucer's *Canterbury Tales* and the Tyll Eulenspiegel stories in Germany tell of bad as well as of good priests.

If the Church was out of step with the changing needs of the world so also was the Empire. The Emperor Sigismund died in 1438 without direct male heirs. The Electors chose in his place Albert of Habsburg, who became Emperor Albert II, a capable and prudent ruler. But he, however, died a year after his accession. He was succeeded in 1440 by his son, Frederick III who reigned as Emperor for fifty-three ineffective years. It is one of the tantalizing episodes of European history that, during that most important second half of the fifteenth century, a central position should have been occupied for fifty-three years by a prince who possessed no outstanding quality save enduring health.

His successor, Maximilian I, was a man of very different stamp. He was capable, ambitious, and energetic. But his ability and energy were chiefly directed towards the expansion of the dominions of the House of Habsburg. His wars and his marriage contracts, arranged for himself and for other members of his family, were all designed for the good of his dynasty. He had acquired, through marriage, an inheritance of the throne of Spain. But even before his death Columbus had carried the flag of Spain to the New World. Maxmilian's grandson, Charles, would succeed to the

33

Habsburg possessions in the Netherlands, Burgundy, Italy, Spain, and the Indies, as well as to the family lands in Austria and Bohemia. Yet the very weight and complexity of the Habsburg family estate would, in the event, make it impossible for the territorial owner to fulfil the traditional role of Emperor.

It was, in fact, for a time not even certain that Charles of Habsburg would succeed his grandfather as Emperor. For, on the death of Maximilian in 1519, the ambitious young King of France, Francis I, made known his candidature for the Imperial throne. The competition of Habsburg and Valois for the votes of the Electors was characterized by bribery on a scale and openness unknown before. In the end the result was largely decided by two men who had not taken bribes, the Elector Duke Frederick of Saxony, surnamed the Wise, and a Welf, the Duke of Brunswick-Wolfenbuttel. Between them they mustered North German sentiment behind Charles. There were at work here the first beginnings of a national feeling. Charles, indeed, had been born in the Netherlands of a Spanish mother, and he was already the King of Spain. Nevertheless he was, at least on the male side, of German stock, the grandson of Maximilian of Habsburg, and to that extent, in North German eyes, to be preferred to a French king.

So in 1519 Charles was elected as Emperor Charles V. For only two years did he rule, even nominally, over his vast domains. Then, in 1521, he made over the Austrian lands to his brother Ferdinand. In 1522 he transferred his court to Spain, and there he remained for seven most important years. For Charles the tug-of-war between Habsburg lands and Imperial duties was to mean incomplete action on either front. In the end the dilemma was to drive him to abdication and withdrawal to a monastery. Eleven years after his first election he was crowned Emperor by the Pope, not at Rome, but at Bologna.

Charlemagne was the first Teutonic Emperor to be crowned in Italy by the Pope. Charles V was the last, seven centuries later. Thereafter a coronation at Frankfurt-on-Main, and not at the hands of the Pope, was the formal assumption of the Imperial dignity.

The second half of the fifteenth century, which had witnessed the discovery of the New World and the opening of the sea route to India, the flowering of the Renaissance and the great glory of Maximilian's Empire, also saw the first stirring of that religious movement which would later be known as the Reformation. Desiderius Erasmus was born at Deventer, in Holland, in 1467, Martin Luther at Eisleben, in Saxony, in 1483, and Ulrich Zwingli in the Canton of St. Gall, in Switzerland, on the first of January, 1448. Even before these there had been men who had preached the need for reform in the Church. John Wycliff in England and John Hus in Bohemia had declaimed against abuses and had demanded better things. Wycliff's followers had been persecuted, Hus had been burned at the stake by order of the Council of Constance, but their influence was still strongly felt in Germany. Many thinking men could see that a reform of the Church was essential; the main question in their minds was whether it could be achieved without schism. Erasmus, for all his great influence on reforming thought, did not leave the Church. He was the leading humanist of his day. His writings directed men's attention to the original text of the Scriptures and to a purer form of worship and Church discipline, free from the superstitions and pedantry which had overlaid the living Church. He was a philosophic and not a dynamic approach.

With Luther, as with Zwingli, the case was different. Moreover, to help Luther there came that sentiment which men now call nationalism. The men of North Germany did not have a high regard for things Italian, and to them the Catholic Church was Italian—it was no longer universal.

The immediate cause of the outbreak of feeling was local and almost fortuitous. It was part of Church doctrine that a repentant evil-doer might appropriately make a gift—of money it might be —to a worthy cause, as evidence of the sincerity of his repentance. But the practice of the trade in Indulgences had degenerated far below the theological theory of Indulgence. Chaucer had written disapprovingly of the Pardoner, with his pardons "comen from Rome al hoot." There was a good deal of hustling business method in this scheme for raising money for the Church's needs. And when one Tetzel, a Dominican friar, came into the bishopric of Magdeburg, in 1517, to raise money for the building of the Cathedral of St. Peter in Rome by the sale of Papal Indulgences he and his assistants used phraseology which linked money payments with the remission of sin in a manner open to very grave abuse, and to a scandalous misconception of what money could do. The whole business greatly offended Martin Luther, by this time Doctor and Professor of Theology at the newly founded University of Wittenberg in Saxony, a man of deep religious conviction supported by a profound knowledge of the Scriptures. He wrote out ninety-five theses, as they have been called in history, ninety-five arguments in Latin, wherein he roundly attacked Tetzel's doings and the whole practice of the sale of papal Indulgences. These theses, on October 31, 1517, he nailed to the Cathedral door at Wittenberg and challenged the learned men of the world to prove him wrong. Luther was a monk of the Augustinian order, and it may have seemed to some, at first, that the affair was no more serious than a dispute over dogma between two monastic orders. Such things had happened before. But a new factor, the printing press, was to affect the dispute. It was only seventy years earlier that Johann Gutenberg had set up his printing press at Mainz. Luther's Reformation was the first movement in the history of the world that had the Press behind it. His theses were printed and distributed all over Germany. The effect was electric. All the humanist impatience with Church formalism, all the popular envy of Church wealth and easy living, all the local opposition to the prince-bishops, all the Northern dislike of the South, all the smouldering antipathies that the Church in Germany had been too blind or too proud to recognize, all these suddenly found their spokesman in this Saxon professor who had dared to challenge so openly an emissary carrying papal credentials. Very quickly Luther found supporters, some of them in high places. Summoned before Cardinal Cajetan at Augsburg in 1518, Luther refused to withdraw his theses. But now he went much further. In 1520 he issued his address to the Christian nobility of the German nation. This address was written in the German tongue. That was something new. Previous religious discussions had been in Latin. Now Martin Luther wrote to his fellow-countrymen in their own language. The address attacked abuses in the Church, advocated doctrinal reforms, and called for a German national Church, independent of Rome.

From the point of view of the Catholic Church, Luther's heresy was now manifest, and a Papal Bull of Excommunication was issued. On December 10, 1520, Luther, having given previous warning of his intention, burned the Papal Bull before an assembly of professors and students in the street before the Elsterthor of the City of Wittenberg. There could hardly have been a more open act of defiance. Charles V, the Emperor, was now in the third year of his reign, profoundly aware of his great responsibilities, and he summoned Luther to appear before the Imperial Diet at Worms. Luther went, assured of the Emperor's safe conduct. Challenged in the presence of the Emperor and his brother Ferdinand to retract his position, he refused to do so. He was allowed to go in safety, but was put under the ban of the Empire by the Edict of Worms. On his return he was intercepted by agents of his protector, the Elector of Saxony, and taken, for his own safety, to the Castle of Wartburg. While there he commenced his translation of the New Testament into German. In fact, neither the Imperial Edict nor the Papal Bull could be enforced against Luther, for he had the support of the countryside. In a very special way he reflected the spirit of the land in which he lived. With his tremendous vitality, his courage, his love of music and poetry, his rough, almost coarse, humour, he was the personification of the North German peasantry. When he wrote the translation of the Bible into German, using for his purpose the High German as spoken in the court of his patron, the

Electoral Prince of Saxony, he fixed the form of classical German for future generations.

The very speed of the spread of Luther's teachings across Northern and Central Germany and into Scandinavia was a measure of the lack of reverence for the old faith. For there was no great disturbance, no persecution. Parish priests took the decision to change their form of service from the Latin Mass to the service in the German tongue without any great excitement among their flock. A Catholic Bishop of Bremen died and was succeeded by a Protestant Bishop, without any marked public comment. Often it seemed as if the main outward sign of the change was that the extensive Church lands were seized by princes or by the cities and that priests and bishops took to themselves lawfully wedded wives.

Far to the south of Saxony another reforming movement had commenced, more dogmatic than Lutheranism and more strongly in contrast to Catholic doctrine and practice. This Swiss reforming movement was led by Ulrich Zwingli, at Zurich. It was to be greatly strengthened by the advent of the French divine John Calvin of Geneva. It was this stream of reforming thought, later to be known as Calvinism, which spread up the Rhine Valley and gained adherents in Württemberg and the Black Forest. Unfortunately for the whole history of the Reformation, Luther and Zwingli were unable to reach agreement at a famous meeting at Marburg in 1529 on the doctrine of transubstantiation, the nature of the elements of bread and wine used in the communion service. So Calvinism and Lutheranism became the ancestors of two separate groups of churches, and another problem was added to Germany's spiritual life.

Religious teaching which attacked the existing order of clerical things was likely to lead men to look with anger and discontent at injustice in the social system. The peasantry of Germany were filled with discontent. Their state was wretched. The old feudalism of the Middle Ages had broken down, money values were changing, but the princes and nobles were unwilling or unable to realize the need for new conditions. So the Peasants' War broke out in 1524, accompanied by a good deal of radical religious teaching. At first the peasants achieved the success of surprise, but the nobles brought mercenary forces into the struggle and the peasantry were defeated by better trained soldiers. The revolt was stamped out with merciless severity indeed—with a display of cruelty which had, so far, been absent from the Reformation in Germany. Although the peasants had been stimulated by the teachings of the reformers and although some of the peasant leaders claimed religious sanction for their uprising, Martin Luther sided strongly with the nobility. He denounced the insurgent peasantry in terms so savage as to seem discordant to us. Without doubt Luther saw clearly the danger to which the Reformation would be exposed if, in the minds of the mass of people, it became associated with mob law. Yet, indeed, already by his close association with the princes and especially with the rulers of Saxony and Hesse, Luther was beginning that administrative connexion between Church and State which has historically characterized Lutheranism in Germany, and has not in every respect worked to the advantage of Church or people.

Frederick the Wise of Saxony had died in 1525, and it was his successor, John, who carried out, soon after his accession, the constitution of a Saxon State Church in the Lutheran doctrine. His colleague of Hesse acted in somewhat the same way. At the first Diet of Speyer—or, in the English spelling, Spires—in 1526, these princes, with the Dukes of Brunswick-Luneburg and of Mecklenburg, the Prince of Anhalt-Kothen, the Count of Mansfeld, and the City of Magdeburg, obtained from the Emperor—represented by his brother Duke Ferdinand—certain recognition of the position of the Lutheran states. Three years later, at the Second Diet of Speyer in 1529, the Emperor, stronger since his victory over France, withdrew the privileges granted. Thereupon the Lutheran states joined in a formal protest and coined thereby a historic word. Six princes and fourteen Imperial Free Cities signed the protest. The history of the next twenty-five years in Germany is the history of the attempt of the Emperor Charles V to stamp out Protestantism, efforts continually interrupted by the demands on his time and resources by events outside Germany.

The Protestant leaders of Northern and middle Germany joined in a League called after the small town Schmalkald. So when at last in 1546 the Emperor Charles V commenced his attempt by warlike means to overcome the Protestant princes it was called the Schmalkaldic War.

At first the Imperial armies were completely victorious. Charles led his army in person against the Elector of Saxony and brought with him the Duke of Alva, his famous general, and the Spanish veterans of his war with France. By the middle of 1547 Charles was master of Germany; only the free city of Magdeburg held out. But his power was not sufficient to accomplish his dual aim, the restoration of the Catholic faith and the overthrow of the great princes. By 1552, he had lost his hold on Germany. Weary of the fruitless struggle, he handed over affairs in Germany to his brother Ferdinand, and it was the latter who made the Peace of Augsburg with the Protestant leaders in 1556. Luther had died in 1546, but the Church which bears his name was by then firmly entrenched in Northern Germany and in Scandinavia.

The Peace of Augsburg laid down a principle, already mooted in an earlier pact, that the territorial prince should decide the religion of his subjects, the principle, as the phrase went, *cujus regio ejus religio*. But no toleration was granted to the individual subjects of a prince. Moreover, it was a treaty between the Catholics and the Lutherans; the Calvinist states were not included. It was, at best, a truce in the struggle, a period of pause in Germany while the religious struggle continued in the Low Countries, in France, and in the British Isles.

Later than in Northern Europe, but influenced by what was happening in Germany, Switzerland, and Holland, England also was becoming Protestant. This was to bring with it, as perhaps had never happened before, an interchange of thought between Britain and Northern Europe. Part of the heritage of today, and one not always realized, lies in the number of hymns and, above all, hymn tunes used in our English Church services which came from the Protestant Churches in Germany and Switzerland. Shakespeare has very few references to Germany in all his plays, but it may be presumed that when he made Prince Hamlet study at the University of Wittenberg he had heard the name of that city through its association with the Professor of Theology, Martin Luther. Together with hymns and tunes there now came from Germany to England some of the basic stories of European literature; up to that date English story-telling had drawn upon Romance, French, Italian, or Classical sources for its plots. Most of the new stories, it is interesting to note, were grim and sombre. One of the first to reach England was the tale of Bishop Hatto, who refused wheat to the starving and was himself devoured by rats. Another was the story of the Wandering Jew. Then came perhaps the greatest of all, the story of Doctor Faustus. And later that group of stories associated with Tyll Eulenspiegel and the "Ship of Fools," mostly stories of satire against clerics or princes, stories which preached the superior good sense and virtue of the common man. It is interesting, at this distance of time, to realize that in Shakespeare's day the English impression of Germany, as derived from the Faustus legend, would be that of a strange combination of deep learning and violent passion.

The religious conflict also led to a commercial link between England and Germany. For Elizabeth of England at the height of her struggle with Spain wished to foster English trade with Northern Europe. Therefore, under her powerful impulse the Company of Merchant Adventurers was founded, and under charter was granted valuable monopolies of trade. In 1587 the Company established its German headquarters in the Hanseatic city of Stade. Thirty years later it moved to the larger city and more commodious harbour of Hamburg. There the Company and its "English House" in the Groningerstrasse remained a feature of

Hamburg life till the Napoleonic wars brought trade with England to a standstill and the Company was dissolved in 1806.

From Luther at the cathedral door at Wittenburg to the outbreak of the Thirty Years War was a period of just over a century. During the whole of the latter part of that century the Catholic Church was earnestly undertaking a reform from within, which should enable it to meet the challenge that had come out of the north. This combined movement, often called the Counter-Reformation, owed much to the inspiration and work of the Jesuits. It was in 1534 that a Spanish nobleman, Don Inigo Lopez de Ricalde y Loyola—usually known as Ignatius Loyola—with three friends, Francis Xavier, Peter Faber, and Iago Lainez, formed the Society of Jesus. Six years later the society received papal approval. Its influence spread rapidly. Its insistence on discipline, obedience, and a careful training in theology made it the rallying force for Catholic piety. In Rome a succession of Popes of ability and high personal character initiated much-needed reforms in the manner of selecting and training priests and bishops.

The Emperor Charles V had wished to call together a great Council of the Church to deal with the problems created by the Reformation movement. It was at his urging that Pope Paul III summoned the Council to meet at Trent, a small city on the main highway south of the Brenner Pass. In fact, the Council of Trent met in three separate sessions, from 1545 to 1547, in 1551–52, and in 1562–3. When the Council first met it was in the minds of many that a compromise over Church doctrine and practice might perhaps be found which would bring back to the Catholic Church many of those who had at first supported the Reformation. The representatives of the French clergy thought in terms of some form of autonomy for a French Catholic Church. As, however, the successive sessions progressed the powerful centralizing influence of the Jesuits, ably led by the skilful arguments of Iago Lainez, gained supremacy. Moreover, by the simple reason of geography, the Italian representation was far more numerous than that of other nations. So, in the end, it was clear that there was to be no compromise and no autonomous national Churches. The doctrines and rules of the Catholic faith were laid down with precision, and the supremacy of the Papacy was proclaimed.

It was also clear that the dynamism of the Jesuits would not be content with purely defensive measures against Protestantism. There would certainly be an attempt to win back lands lost to the Protestants. In the uneasy truce which followed the Peace of Augsburg both sides formed up for battle. The Calvinist princes of Southern Germany formed a "Union." In return the Catholic League was formed under the valuable leadership of Maximilian of Bavaria.

Only the very wisest statecraft could have avoided the appeal to arms. The actual fighting began in Bohemia. Ferdinand of Austria, son of the reigning Emperor, was a pious Catholic, taught by the Jesuits and convinced of his duty to combat heresy. While Prince of Styria he had driven out of his territory the local Protestants. In 1617 he succeeded to the throne of Bohemia. Immediately he met with resistance from the Protestant nobles of Bohemia. Tension grew rapidly worse, and in the spring of 1618, as a result of an altercation, the Protestant group seized two agents sent by Ferdinand and threw them from the windows of the Royal Palace at Prague, an event which became known as the "defenestration." In the next year the Bohemians rejected Ferdinand as their king and offered the throne to the Calvinist Prince Frederick of the Palatinate, who married a daughter of James, King of Scotland and of England. In the same year Ferdinand succeeded to the Empire.

The Calvinists of South Germany supported Frederick of the Palatinate; the Catholic League supported the Emperor Ferdinand II. But the important Lutheran princes of the north were not prepared to bestir themselves to aid a Calvinist. It was the aid given to the Emperor by the Duke of Bavaria which really decided the issue in 1620 and for the next few years. For the troops which Maximilian of Bavaria sent to invade Bohemia were commanded by

43

Johann Tserklaes von Tilly, of Dutch family, one of the great captains of the time. On November 8, 1620, the combined Imperial forces decisively defeated the Bohemians at the battle of the White Mountain, not far from Prague. King Frederick with his English bride fled to Holland, where they faded into retirement, secure, however, of a niche in history, as the parents of Sophia of Hanover, the ancestress of the Hanoverian kings of England. The revolt in Bohemia was suppressed with a harshness that is remembered in that land to this day. Tilly and his Bavarian soldiers moved to the Rhineland, and Frederick's subjects had to pay for their Prince's adventure by the conquest and occupation of the Palatinate by Catholic troops.

At last, however, the Lutheran princes of the north were becoming alarmed for their own safety, and they were receiving encouraging messages from Scandinavia. On the other hand, the Emperor was beginning to feel that it was not satisfactory for his dignity and power that he should, militarily, be so dependent upon Maximilian's Bavarian armies. At this period, in 1625, Count Wallenstein of Friedland, a Catholic from Bohemia, already a famous soldier, came to the Emperor with the proposal that, if the Emperor would provide artillery and arms, he, Wallenstein, would raise an army and would maintain it by the simple process of living off the country. The Emperor accepted the proposal, and to Wallenstein's banner there flocked soldiers of fortune of every nationality—Protestant as well as Catholic—held together by the bond of admiration for a general with unusual gifts of leadership.

In 1626 the Emperor set his forces in motion. With Wallenstein's army on the right and Tilly's Bavarians on the left, the Imperial forces moved northward. Count Mansfeld, the leader of the North German Protestants, attempted to bar the way at the Elbe crossing at Dessau. He was defeated by Wallenstein with heavy loss. King Christian of Denmark, whose son was the Protestant Bishop of Verden, marched into the Weser Valley to help his co-religionists. He was defeated by Tilly at Lutteram-Barenberge, in Brunswick.

None of the Protestant leaders could halt these two great generals. Before long Wallenstein was in Mecklenburg and then deep into Denmark. Tilly was on the Elbe estuary with his headquarters at Stade. But the prosperous Hanseatic city of Hamburg had seen the looming war, and its burghers, with great energy and at heavy cost, had between 1615 and 1625 constructed a huge rampart, with twenty-one bastions, around their city. Tilly had come within sight of this fortress of the north, but he had judged it too strong and had passed by. Stralsund, another Hanseatic city, held out, despite all the assaults of Wallenstein's army. Its citizens were aided in their defence by contingents sent by the King of Sweden and also by Scots. For here comes into the story a link with British history. In October 1626 some 2,000 Scots from the Clan Mackay, under a colonel of the clan name, sailed from Cromarty and Aberdeen to join the army of Count Mansfeld and to fight for the Protestant cause. When they reached Gluckstadt in Holstein Mansfeld had already been defeated. So they took service with the King of Denmark. Some companies were sent to help garrison Bremen, and some, in the course of time, joined the garrison of Stralsund. Later Mackay's regiment took service under Gustavus Adolphus, and that regiment in unbroken descent became the 1st Regiment of Foot in the British Army—The Royal Scots.

In spite of local checks at Hamburg and at Stralsund, the Imperial victory seemed overwhelming. The Emperor had reduced to impotence the Protestants of Northern Germany. Yet the very magnitude of the victory was to prove the beginning of disaster. The leaders of the Catholic League were bitterly jealous of Wallenstein, whom they suspected, with reason, of harbouring personal ambitions at their expense. The exactions of the invading armies, living off the countryside, as Wallenstein had promised, were driving the population to fury and bitter resentment. Indeed, all armies lived off the surrounding towns and villages, but the size of Wallenstein's army, which he refused to disband, made the Imperial cause more and more hated in Northern Germany. Any popular resistance was answered with force and often with great cruelty by the hard-bitten soldiery. Perhaps more important than all, the Imperial successes had aroused strong reactions in France. Richelieu, Minister to King Louis of France, was himself a Cardinal of the Church. On grounds of faith he should have welcomed the success of the Catholic Emperor. But Richelieu was first and foremost a statesman of France, and he was not prepared to see Habsburg power grow too great. So he supported, with a treaty and with money, the campaign undertaken by Gustavus Adolphus, King of Sweden.

Under pressure from the Catholic League Ferdinand dismissed Wallenstein. Already, however, Gustavus Adolphus had landed in Pomerania, with 13,000 Swedish troops. Tilly, now in command of all the Imperial forces, marched out of the Weserland to meet the new foe, capturing and sacking the city of Magdeburg (1631) on his way. At Breitenfeld, near Liepzig, in Saxony, the two armies met, and Gustavus Adolphus won a definite victory. The Swedish army marched southward. Frankfurt-on-Main, Darmstadt, Mainz, and finally Munich was entered by the Swedes, and it seemed that even Vienna itself was threatened. Tilly had suffered a further heavy defeat and had died of his wounds in 1632. In desperation the Emperor recalled Wallenstein. At the battle of Lutzen, in Saxony, although victory in the end went to the Swedish soldiers, Gustavus Adolphus was killed in the hour of triumph. There had been no real reconciliation between Wallenstein and the Emperor. The general was again dismissed. He withdrew to Bohemia. But he was not trusted. It was suspected that he was plotting to regain power, and he was assassinated by a conspiracy of officers.

The genius of leadership had departed from both sides, but the struggle dragged on. No longer was it a war of religious principles. It was a war to decide whether France should have Alsace and Lorraine or whether Sweden should gain territory on the south shore of the Baltic. Armies drawn from almost every race in Europe marched backward and forward across Germany, quartering themselves upon the population, plundering for food for man and beast, hated and feared by peasant and townsman, and repaying hatred by cruelty and destruction. In all Germany there were only two important cities which were not occupied by a hostile army at some time or other during the Thirty Years War. They were Vienna and Hamburg. The whole land of Germany sank into a degradation of cruelty and wretchedness. It was a part of the evil of the times that a hysteria of witch-hunting swept the country, whereby thousands of victims were put to death.

Historians of the time were so horrified by the tragedy that they possibly exaggerated the figures of loss of population. Even conservative figures, however, suggest that Germany had about 21 million inhabitants before the war started and about $13\frac{1}{2}$ million in 1648. Parts of Saxony and Mecklenburg were almost depopulated, and villages and their lands decayed to destruction because there was no one left to work.

In the end it was exhaustion and not victory for either side that brought the war to a close. For five long years delegates wrangled in the city of Osnabruck to try to negotiate a settlement. Finally, on October 24, 1648, the Treaty of Westphalia was signed. A disastrous war had been brought to an end, but the price of peace was the fragmentation of Germany. Nor, when it was all over, was the relative position of Protestant and Catholic on the map of Germany very different from what it had been at the time of the Peace of Augsburg.

By 1648 in most of the great countries of Europe the powerful forces of Reformation and Counter-Reformation had worked out a definite result. The Scandinavian lands, with England and Scotland and Holland, were Protestant, with a Protestant ruling house. Poland, Italy, Spain, and France were Catholic. Only in Germany was the country still divided, with Catholic areas and Protestant areas, as it is divided today. Germany is certainly not a land of religious bigotry, and the two religious communities respect each other's feelings. Yet the fact remains that there is in Germany today a "confessional problem"—the fact that two large religious communities, Catholic and Protestant, live side by side in one country. The existence of this problem must not be ignored nor its importance minimized.

CHAPTER FOUR

AUSTRIA AND PRUSSIA; HANOVER AND FRANCE
(1648–1789)

On October 24, 1648, the church bells of Osnabruck rang to celebrate the signing of the Treaty of Westphalia, the last great international treaty to be written in Latin. The deliberations had lasted five long years. Most of the nations, large and small, of continental Europe had taken part in the discussions, and the eventual outcome was a triumph of petty jealousies. The terms of the Treaty of Westphalia were designed to alter the map of Germany both on its frontiers and at its very centre. Switzerland and the Dutch Netherlands, countries which had already won their independence in the field, were now legally independent of the Empire. Alsace and Lorraine went to France. Bohemia became part of the Empire, with the provision that its Protestant inhabitants should have the right to their religion. Sweden gained what she had fought for—the North German province of Western Pomerania and the secularized bishoprics of Bremen and Verden. The old contest between Bavaria and the Palatinate for the elector's hat was settled by creating an eighth electorate and giving it to Bavaria. Brandenburg gained part of Pomerania, and the important and now secularized bishoprics of Minden and Halberstadt. Every one of the German Reichsfursten, the Princes of the Empire, received in the Treaty of Westphalia the right to make foreign treaties, so long as they were not directed against the Empire. Furthermore, it was specifically laid down that, in any matter where religious questions might be

49

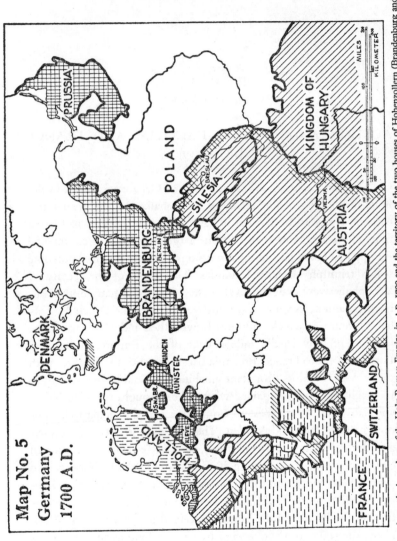

Map No. 5
Germany
1700 A.D.

The map shows the boundary of the Holy Roman Empire in A.D. 1700 and the territory of the two houses of Hohenzollern (Brandenburg and Prussia and Hapsburg (Austria). France had gained Alsace by the Treaty of Ryswick, 1697. The Hohenzollerns had commenced to acquire territory in western Germany, partly by inheritance and partly by the Treaty of Westphalia, 1648. The title of King of Prussia was assumed in 1701. In 1742 Frederick the Great seized Silesia from Austria.

involved, the Protestant and Catholic Princes of the Empire had the right to deliberate in two separate bodies.

Four centuries earlier it had, for one brief moment, appeared that a great German chieftain might arise to rule over the German peoples, as the Plantagenets and the Capets were to rule over Englishmen and Frenchmen.

Even as late as the days of the Emperor Maximilian I there had been a fleeting chance that the Emperor and the electors might have forged a workable constitution, at least for the German portion of the Holy Roman Empire. That faint hope was shattered by the hammer strokes of Martin Luther as he nailed his theses to the cathedral door at Wittenberg.

The mirage of the Imperial Dream and the savagery of the religious wars had reduced the medieval Germany of the Welfs and the Hohenstaufens to a hotchpotch of petty principalities. As the result of the Treaty of Westphalia no less than three hundred and fifty units of government were scattered about Germany, each one possessing almost independent sovereignty. The shattering effect can be studied in a part of the country known to many Britons. In the area comprised within the former British Zone there are today five constituent states of the Federal German Republic. They are Schleswig-Holstein, Hamburg, Bremen, Lower Saxony, and North Rhine-Westphalia. In 1648 within the same area there were forty-nine states, and though they owed a shadowy allegiance to an Empire and an Imperial Diet, they were, for most practical purposes, masters of their own internal and external affairs. In Thuringia and the middle Rhine the fragmentation was as thorough. Only in the south were the somewhat larger states of Bavaria and Württemberg, and to the east there were Brandenburg and Austria.

The Thirty Years War had been disastrous for the citizens and the yeomen. The men who had best survived the terrible time had been the small local chiefs who had commanded their own mercenary troops. The civic councils and farmers' meetings which had given a democratic background, of a sort, to the Germany of the

Middle Ages were swept away. The land was ruled by scores of petty autocrats. Each had his little court with its ceremonies and its local privileges. Over all these princes glittered the splendour of the court of Versailles. For fashions came from France. In the latter half of the seventeenth century and throughout the days of the eighteenth until the onset of the French Revolution of the kingdom of France was by far the most powerful and wealthy state in Europe. So long as French diplomacy could hold in check the danger of a union between Spain and Austria, France, with its fertile soil, intelligent population, its men of science and learning, easily over-shadowed all other realms in Europe.

It has been argued in defence of these pocket kingdoms and their local rulers that they did serve to rescue the country from the complete breakdown which threatened after the Thirty Years War. It is indeed true that many of the princes were good adminis-trators and brave soldiers. Many worked hard to restore the econ-omy of their countryside. But even this hard work was utterly local in its outlook. Taken as a whole, they were a sterile and in-effective group, as, indeed, was to be expected by the narrow boun-daries of their territory and the artificial rules of their existence. Indeed, one result of this period was the extreme formalism of the German social system which has endured into our own century. Elaborate court ceremonial, rigid orders of precedence, family pride and prejudice elevated to a caste system, permeated the streets and squares of the smallest city. Most of the princely families had their own orders of chivalry, their own commissions as generals, colonels and captains, and their own warrants of appointment to positions in and around the court. To this day there is sung or whistled the pleasant melody about the state of Lippe Detmold, which had a general, a captain, a sergeant-major, but only one soldier—who went to the war and got killed. But that is only an exaggerated description of what occurred over the whole of Wes-tern and Central Germany in the seventeenth and eighteenth cen-turies. Of patriotic German feeling there was very little trace.

These princes were ready to join sides with foreign Powers and to accept foreign money for doing it, French money or English money. The Grand Duke of Hesse raised soldiers among his peasantry for English money, and shipped them to America to fight in a quarrel in which they had little interest.

Partly as a result of the multiplication of small courts and the resultant formalism, there grew up in Germany a marked Stratification of society and a strong class-consciousness. The landed gentry, the armed forces, the officials and the professional classes had each their own pride of place and a rigid code of social behaviour. The professional middle class, whether well-to-do or impoverished, guarded jealously its privileged status. Such a middle class was conservative, traditional, and, especially in Prussia, monarchist. It survived the shock of the French Revolution. It survived the liberal movement of 1848. It was hard hit by the defeat of 1918 and by the flight of Kaiser William II; it was hit harder still, perhaps, by the inflation of 1922. Yet it still influences German political and social thought.

The Peace of Westphalia had splintered classical Germany. If there were to be again a centralizing force it was hardly to be looked for in the lands between the Elbe and the Rhine. Only to the east were there two units large enough to play a part in the history of Europe. Men would soon begin to use the titles "Prussia" and "Austria."

Both these states had grown up as border marches against a heathen east. Austria had to face and fight the Turks, Brandenburg the Slavs.

What men later called Prussia was in fact the marriage of two quite separate territorial institutions, the old March of Brandenburg and the land of the Teutonic Knights. A previous chapter has told of the eastward move of the Saxons. It was as early as A.D. 928 that Henry the Fowler at the head of his Saxons in winter crossed the frozen river Havel and stormed the Wendish fortress of Brandibor. This Germanic penetration into Slav territory was short-lived, for the Saxon settlement was plundered and burnt, and for some two centuries the township remained in Slav hands. It was not until 1134 that Albert the Bear founded the Nordmark and established his capital at Brandenburg. North and south of Brandenburg, Saxon settlers, men from Westphalia and even farther west, moved into the new lands, fighting the Slavs, establishing their Saxon villages, but never completely driving out the Slav inhabitants. Right up to the days before the First World War a Slav dialect, Wendisch, was spoken in a wide area south of Berlin, and recently Russian advisers to the East German Government have revived this Slav tongue. An earlier chapter has already told how the Brandenburg inheritance fell into the hands of the Emperor Sigismund, and how he gave his title to his friend, Frederick of Nuremburg, from the House of Hohenzollern in South Germany. According to legend Berlin was founded in 1237, and Frankfurt-on-the-Oder about 1250.

About this same time, much farther east, on the shores of the Baltic, another area of German influence was being established. Already, during the crusades, a religious order of German knights had come into being in the Holy Land. Their headquarters and a hospital were established at Acre. In the latter part of the thirteenth century this Order of Teutonic Knights (Deutscher Ritterorden) was invited by the Polish Duke Conrad of Masovia to move to the south shores of the Baltic to aid him in his struggle against a heathen tribe. He allotted to the Order lands in the district of Kulm on the lower Vistula. The heathen lived in the forests and sandy hills of the Baltic coast lands east of that great river. Their name was written in the early chronicles as Prusai, whence in English Prussian, in High German Preussen and in German Court Latin Borussii. The Knights were rapidly victorious. Wherever their forces penetrated they established walled castles to secure their gains against counter-attack from Poland and Lithuania. Such strongholds were Thorn, Culm, Marienwerder, and Graudenz. Finally Marienburg, the great central stronghold of the Order, was built in the year 1272. Danzig was won by the Order in 1310, and they spread their influence over

Pomerellen, the lands south of Danzig on the westward side of the Vistula. In the wake of the Military Knights came traders and settlers; but the Knights themselves were a religious order, sworn to chastity and therefore not a territorial aristocracy. For a time they held sway over a large stretch of country along the southern shores of the Baltic, but there came steadily increasing pressure from the rising Polish kingdom. The Lithuanians had become Christian by the fourteenth century and thereafter tended to make common cause with the Poles against the Order. Already it had become involved in trade and land-owning and had become weakened by internal disputes.

At the battle of Tannenberg in 1410 the Grand Master and his Knights were defeated by a combined Polish and Lithuanian army. The Order lost Danzig, lost Pomerellen and Thorn and Culm. Later, by the Treaty of Thorn in 1466, the Order had to surrender West Prussia to King Casimir of Poland and was allowed to hold East Prussia as a fief from the Polish crown. Only in the lands round their great fortress of Konigsberg did the Order still maintain its position as an island of Germanic influence, separated by a hundred or more miles from the remainder of Germany.

In 1512 the office of Grand Master of the Order was vacant. Maximilian I, the Emperor, supported successfully the candidature of a junior member of the House of Hohenzollern, Albert of Brandenburg. The effect of his action would have surprised Maximilian had he lived to see it. Thirteen years later, six years after Maximilian's death, Albert of Brandenburg, after a talk with Martin Luther at Wittenberg, decided to accept the Lutheran teaching and practice and to bring the whole Order in his wake. This meant far more than a change of religious faith—it meant that what had once been a monastic order of soldier monks was to become a group of landowning families, that the Grand Master would become the Duke of Prussia, that he would marry and found a family, and that the head of the new Dukedom would be a Hohenzollern. Within a century that newly formed Dukedom was left without a male heir.

History was made when the heiress, Anne of Prussia, gave her hand to her relative the Markgrave of Brandenburg. The frontier lands of the north and east came together in one family, and the isolated group of Germans around Konigsberg were strengthened by their dynastic alliance with a rising and Protestant Brandenburg.

Frederick William, surnamed "the Great Elector," ruled Brandenburg from 1640 to 1688. The Treaty of Westphalia had added important, but often distant, territories to his dominions. But the war had terribly impoverished the land. His prudent and wise conduct of affairs during his long reign improved the economy and added further lands to the House of Hohenzollern. Among the wisest of his acts was the granting of asylum to the Huguenots. In 1685 King Louis of France revoked the Edict of Nantes. That Edict had given freedom of worship and political guarantees to the Huguenots. Now that their freedom of public worship was lost many decided to emigrate. Frederick William offered them sanctuary in Brandenburg. Some 20,000 settled in his territory, bringing technical ability, industry, and man-power to a countryside devastated by war. At the end of the century almost one-third of the total population of Berlin was made up of these Huguenot settlers. They repaid the hospitality offered to them by producing many capable and distinguished servants of the Prussian House, and perhaps by contributing a valuable ingredient to the strongly individual character of the people of Berlin.

Brandenburg had early accepted the Lutheran teaching, Grand Master Albert had taken the German Order from Catholicism to Protestantism, and the Huguenots had brought Calvinism with them. The day would come when the Kingdom of Prussia would be the leading Protestant state in continental Europe.

As yet, however, it was not a kingdom. Frederick William was Elector of Brandenburg and Duke of Prussia. Titles within the boundaries of the Holy Roman Empire could be bestowed only by the Emperor himself. But Prussia lay outside the boundaries of the Empire. So in 1701 Frederick, son of the Great Elector, caused himself to be crowned "King in Prussia" at Konigsberg, well outside the Imperial frontiers. The Emperor Leopold I acquiesced, but he did not bestow the title. Frederick was still Elector of Brandenburg, but the greater title overshadowed the lesser, and before long the ruler from the Alte Schloss in Berlin was generally called the King of Prussia, and the name of Prussia, derived from a small heathen tribe on the Baltic shores, spread across the breadth of Germany till it reached the Rhine and the Ruhr.

Hundreds of miles to the south of Berlin the other great frontier kingdom was taking shape after the settlement of the Treaty of Westphalia. The history of Austria and of its capital city, Vienna, differed in many respects from the picture in Northern Germany. The heartland of Austria had long been part of the Roman Empire. The province of Noricum was conquered by Caesar Augustus. Its population was Celtic. As was the case in Gaul and in Britain, the Celts became Romanized, adopted Roman speech and culture. Vindobona was established as a Roman station on the Danube; in later years it would be called Wien by its inhabitants, Vienna by the English. Centuries later the Ostrogoths invaded the land and settled amid the Romano-Celtish people. Then the Ostrogoths moved on westwards, and the flood-tide of wandering Slav tribes came into Carinthia and Lower Austria, to use the terms of today. But in the eleventh and twelfth centuries the tide commenced to flow the other way. Cistercian monks and Bavarian settlers brought German muscle and German culture eastward until they reached the Karawanken Alps and the line of the river Leitha south-east of Vienna. There they halted, for they were faced to the east by the Avars (also called Magyars or Hungarians), and to the south-east by Slav peoples, Croats, and Slovenes.

At first the land was under Bavarian control; indeed, it was called the Bayrische Ostmark. Then, in 1282, the family of Habsburg, coming from the neighbourhood of Zürich, established control of the Ostmark, soon to be known as Osterreich or Austria. The family had already given one Emperor to the succession,

Emperor Rudolph in 1273. There was to be another, the Emperor Albert, in 1298. In a few years the family had added Styria to their possessions, and a few years later Carinthia.

By the fifteenth century the House of Habsburg possessed in the south-east corner of the Empire a compact group of family domains. The Emperor Sigismund died without male issue in 1438. His son-in-law, Albert II of Habsburg, was elected to succeed to the title. He reigned only one year. There followed his son, Frederick III, who occupied the Imperial throne without distinction for fifty-three years. Then came the Emperor Maximilian I, with whose reign commenced that glorious but short-lived period of greatness which would see the House of Habsburg ruling over great territories in two continents. He had in some measure a conception of the medieval meaning of the Imperial title, but his wars, and the marriages he arranged, were, as we have already seen, for the betterment of the House of Habsburg and not for the salvation of the Holy Roman Empire. Austrian historians look to Maximilian as the founder of the Austrian army.

His grandson, Charles V, when elected Emperor, was ruler by marriage and by his father's conquests over Austria, the Netherlands, Burgundy, much of Italy, Spain and, so far as rule was possible, over the Spanish Indies. But this great state was to last just two years. Then he made over the traditional Habsburg lands to his brother Ferdinand. For years Charles lived in Spain, and in Spain he died. At his death his Spanish and Netherlands possessions went to his son Philip, the Austrian possessions to his brother Ferdinand. The Spanish and Austrian branches of the house of Habsburg never came together again. However, the Austrian branch at least extended its own terrain. For in 1525 Bohemia, Moravia, and Silesia were acquired.

During the Thirty Years War the Austrian house of Habsburg had been the mainstay of the Catholic cause in middle Europe. When the war came to an end with the Peace of Westphalia that position stood unchallenged. But the prestige of the Emperor was greatly weakened. Because the Emperor was bound to be a Habsburg and therefore a Catholic, the princes of the Protestant north would be hostile, lukewarm, or friendly, as it suited them, but they would bear little loyalty to the tradition of the Emperor as such.

Yet something was to happen which would bring back memories of the Imperial Dream. In 1685 Vienna was besieged by the Turks. The Ottoman Turks had overrun the Balkans, captured Crete and Cyprus, swept over the plains of Hungary, and now their army was hammering at the gates of the capital of the Empire. For a brief period Vienna was the citadel of the Christian West. The citizens resisted bravely, though they were hard pressed. Jan Sobieski, King of Poland, brought his cavalry from the north, Charles of Lorraine led a Bavarian army from the west, the Turks were driven from the walls of Vienna, and the danger was past. But for many a decade the battle with the Turks and the gradual reconquest of South-east Europe was to be the dominant issue for Vienna and the Austrians. British readers of history associate Prince Eugene of Savoy with the battle of Blenheim and the great comradeship of arms with the Duke of Marlborough. To Austrian history he is the brilliant general who captured Belgrade from the Turks.

Vienna was a city which looked east and south. Slav, Magyar, Italian influences, even Turkish influences, combined to produce an atmosphere and a culture which was very different from that of the northern rival, Berlin.

Such were Austria and Prussia as they emerged from the disaster of the Thirty Years War. Two other German states deserve mention. Bavaria had been ruled by the House of Wittelsbach from the year 1180. The same family would, indeed, continue to reign in Munich until the abolition of the Bavarian monarchy in 1918. Through its devotion to the Catholic faith the House of Wittelsbach had played a dominant, perhaps even a decisive, part in the early days of the Reformation. At a time when the Lutheran confession was spreading rapidly over Northern Germany, and when Duke Ulrich of Wurtemberg was accepting Calvinist teaching,

59

Duke William IV of Bavaria opposed the Reformation and brought Jesuit teachers to the national university of Ingolstadt in the year 1549. Some seventy years later his successor Duke Maximilian I put himself at the head of the Catholic League and sent his Bavarian troops, under their famous general Tilly, to defeat Frederick and his Bohemian army at that battle of the White Mountain to which we have already referred.

During the Thirty Years War Bavaria was the battle ground of contesting armies, and the Swedes under Gustavus Adolphus marched into Munich. In the end the Duchy emerged from the conflict with the added dignity of the Elector's hat and with a tradition of absolute monarchism closely associated with the Catholic Church. Moreover, even in the days of conflict, rulers such as Albert V and Maximilian I had established that tradition of support for art, architecture, and culture which is ever associated with the name of the House of Wittelsbach.

Far to the north the landowning squires of the House of Welf were working out a destiny strangely different from the cultured monarchs of Bavaria. In the far-off days when Henry II was King of England and Thomas a Becket was slain in Canterbury Cathedral, Henry the Lion, of the House of Welf, reigned at Brunswick and held within his Dukedom of Saxony most of the territory which today forms Land Niedersachsen. The Duke fought with the Emperor Barbarossa and was defeated. The great Duchy was broken up and all that remained to the House of Welf were the old family lands whose boundaries are, roughly, within the triangle formed by Luneberg, Brunswick, and Hanover. The Bishopric of Hildesheim was independent; the city of Goslar was a Free City of the Empire and the centre of Imperial faction against the Welfs.

In the family of Welf, as in many other princely houses of Germany, the rule of primogeniture did not apply. Each son of the family expected to have a part of the family estate allotted to him for his maintenance. The family history of the years 1200 to 1600 is therefore of a continual splitting and regrouping; splitting when there were many sons, regrouping by marriage or when the male line died out. The family holdings did, however, tend to crystallize into three main estates whose outlines are with us today. First there was the Duchy of Brunswick-Wolfenbuttel; then there was the Duchy of Brunswick-Luneberg; and finally the Duchy of Brunswick-Kalemburg, covering the lands of Hanover, Nienstedt, Springe, and Hamelin. The castle was at Kalemburg, slightly east of the main road to Göttingen.

In fact, however, even in the House of Welf there was a realization that this endless splitting of the patrimony could be overdone. Thus came the quaint story of the seven sons of Duke William of Luneburg, who assembled in Celle on December 3, 1610, after the death of their father, and decided that the whole estate should go in the first instance to the eldest son, and that he should pay the others an allowance. They made a further decision, and this was curious. They agreed that only one of the seven should marry and that this should not necessarily be the eldest son; it should be decided by lot. The winner of the lottery was George, the second youngest. He accordingly married the daughter of the Duke of Hesse, settled down in Schloss Harzburg, and became in due course the ancestor of the Kings of Great Britain and of Hanover.

His happy life in Harzburg was rudely interrupted by the outbreak of the Thirty Years War. George of Luneburg fought for the Protestant cause and proved himself a brave soldier and a good general. By reason of the unquiet times he moved the family residence from Kalemburg to Hanover, till then a small town of little importance, and he built the Leine Palace in the centre of the city. He died in 1641 before the wars came to an end, leaving an eldest son of nineteen and three younger sons, whereof the youngest was Ernst August, destined to be the father of the King of England.

James VI of Scotland and I of England had a daughter, beautiful and popular, who married Frederick, Elector Palatine. After her husband's bid for the throne of Bohemia and his defeat at the White Mountain they withdrew to safety and retirement in the

Netherlands. There they had a large family, of whom the youngest was a girl, Sophia, born in 1650. She grew up to be beautiful and talented and was sought in marriage by many princes. Apparently the only one who really engaged her affections was George William, the second of the four sons of George of Luneburg. He had visited her in Holland, accompanied by his younger brother, Ernst August. A marriage was arranged between George and Sophia. Then George had second thoughts. He discussed the matter with his younger brother and wrote a document, a Renunciation of Marriage, three hundred words long. He arranged it should be Ernst August, his younger brother, who should marry Sophia. The lady no doubt felt piqued, but she was twenty-eight by this time and was not happy at her mother's court. "A good establishment is all I care for, and if this is secured by the younger brother, the choice is a matter of indifference to me." Ernst August was twenty-nine, Sophia twenty-eight when they were married at Heidelberg in the autumn of 1658. They returned to Hanover and took up residence with the elder brother, George William, in the Schloss Leine. Thus in the person of the youngest of twelve children came to the House of Welf the first faint claim to the English throne. Their son George Louis was born in 1660. The throne of England looked very far away from a crib in the Schloss Leine.

Forty years later the scene had dramatically changed. Ernst August the father had been a careful, shrewd dynast. He had carried through an Act of Primogeniture, whereby the whole of the family estates were to go eventually to his son George Louis. He had secured the Elector's hat for Hanover. Ernst August died in 1698. Now George Louis was beginning to appear a person of some importance. He was Elector of Hanover, possessor of the Brunswick-Kalemburg lands and heir to his ageing uncle, George William, ruler of Brunswick-Luneberg. Moreover, his mother was a potential claimant to the throne of England. For to the Protestants of England Sophia, Protestant granddaughter of James I, had become a person of great importance. William and Mary had no children;

Anne's last surviving child, the little Duke of Gloucester, died of smallpox. All other Stuart heirs were Catholic. So in 1701 the Act of Succession was passed by Parliament at Westminster, naming as heir to the throne of England, after Anne, the Electress Sophia and the heirs of her body.

So for a further dozen years the drama was played out. In the foreground were two women. One the sickly, middle-aged, rather tragic Queen Anne of England. The other an imperious veteran in her eighties, the Dowager Electress Sophia, playing the *grande dame* to perfection at Hanover, discussing theology and philosophy with Leibnitz, carrying on a voluminous correspondence with relatives all over Europe, planning the cultivation of oranges, apples, and pineapples in the great orangery at Herrenhausen, tiring out her ladies-in-waiting with her vivacity and energy, and ever dreaming of the day when she would write herself "Sophia, Queen of England." In the background were two men. One was Sophia's son, George Louis, self-centred, cynical, brave, a rather humdrum little man, but no fool, carefully exact in his accounts, close in many matters, unlovable, and a bit coarse in his tastes. The other was James Stuart, son to King James II, good-looking, honest and upright, rather dull in wit, who really settled the whole matter when he wrote in March 1714 three letters, to Queen Anne, to Lord Oxford, and to Lord Bolingbroke, to make it quite clear that he would not give up his Catholic faith even for the throne of England.

In the end fate cheated Sophia. For she died in her eighty-fifth year, just four months before the death of Queen Anne. So, by a series of events which ever surprised him, George, Elector of Hanover, became King of England.

The union of Hanover and England was personal to the monarch. There was neither a joint Privy Council nor joint administration. From the point of view of Hanover the union brought more trouble than advantage, for it meant that Hanover was henceforward involved in England's great struggle against France for colonial supremacy. As far as London society was concerned the Hanoverian connexion brought with it an interesting shift in English dynastic links. Whereas before 1714 there had been scarcely one German princess on the throne of England, after that date there was to be a continuous stream of brides coming from the smaller German states to grace the British Court. Partly by reason of these princely marriages travel to Germany became fashionable among Englishmen of wealth. Young gentlemen of quality, such as James Boswell, who set off on the Grand Tour in Europe liked to include a visit to two or three small German courts. There their vanity was flattered by being treated as equals by persons of high-sounding titles of nobility. Men of learning, like Dr. Thomas Nugent, found in the libraries of the German noble houses early examples of printing and works of science which were rare and interesting. These early visitors have left journals of their travellings which record shocking roads, simple inns, but elaborate court ceremonial and pleasant life in the small towns.

Linked with the personal union but by no means dependent upon it was another development of great interest to the history of the British Army. "The force voted by Parliament for the campaign of 1703 consisted, as in the previous years, of 18,000 British and 22,000 Germans." This is a quotation from the opening words of Chapter II of Book VI in Fortescue's standard *History of the British Army*. For over a century British and Germans were to fight side by side not only in Germany but almost everywhere that British troops fired and fought. The history of joint action on the soil of Germany itself commences with the campaign of Blenheim in 1703, and finishes with the small action at Gorde, near Luneburg, on September 16, 1813. At Bleinheim not only was there an Imperial army under Prince Eugene which fought alongside an army under the great British Duke of Marlborough, there was even combined action within Marlborough's command. Lord Cutt's Division which attacked the village of Blenheim was drawn up in column of four brigades. The first was Row's British brigade, the second was

Hanoverian, the third was Fergusson's British brigade, and the fourth was Hessian.

Those who, with historical backing, accuse the German people of being warlike and fond of fighting, should therefore, in fairness also remember that for more than a century it was English gold which made it possible for many Germans to indulge in war. To readers of today who may be inclined to think of these soldiers as having been employed after the fashion of the Foreign Legion, with British officers and German rank and file, it should be explained that, on the contrary, national contingents served under their own officers and indeed under their own generals. For example, in 1746, at the time of the campaign against Charles Edward Stuart, the Young Pretender, the five thousand Hessian troops who were brought over to Scotland to garrison Perth and block the way from the Highlands to the south were under the command of their own royal Prince, Frederick of Hesse Cassel.

The whole of the eighteenth century is full of records of combined British and German forces fighting as allies in Europe. At Dettingen, in South Germany, in 1743 King George II of England commanded a mixed force of British and Austrian troops. At Minden in 1759 Duke Ferdinand of Brunswick gained a notable victory with an allied army of British, Hanoverian, Brunswick, and Prussian soldiers. Outside Germany, Hessian and Hanoverian troops fought as part of British formations in America, in the Spanish Peninsula, and the Low Countries. Partly through this close association on the battlefield, partly through the military fame of King Frederick the Great, of Prussia, there was a noticeable infiltration of German ideas of dress, drill, and, to some extent, tactics into British army thought.

As for the campaigns themselves, they often had little enough to do with the real interests of the country folk over whose fields the armies marched. Southey's poem "The Battle of Blenheim" has the well-remembered lines:

" 'Now tell us about the war,
And what they fought each other for . . .'
'Why, that I cannot tell,' said he;
'But 'twas a famous victory.' "

Eighteenth-century farmers and burghers on the Weser and the
Lippe and the Werra must often have had similar feelings. It was
good statecraft that led William Pitt the Elder to claim in Parliament that his policy would conquer Canada on the plains of Germany, but the citizens of Bielefeld or Dortmund, who had to put
up with the comings and goings of strange armies, would hardly
see the force of that argument.

One example of the way in which those who had nothing to do
with the struggle were swept into the maelstrom may be quoted.
During the 1759 campaign the French armies captured Frankfurt-
on-Main, in order to use the city as a base and to secure the important bridgehead over the river Main. But Frankfurt was an Imperial
Free City and, in the thought of the day, entitled to privileges of
neutrality. The allies, led by bad example, seized in their turn the
Free Hanseatic City of Bremien, to gain a base on the Weser.

Though much of this fighting on German soil during the
eighteenth century had to do with the question of the Spanish
succession or the rivalry of Britain and France in India or the New
World, there was one series of campaigns which did vitally concern the history of Germany. This was the struggle between
Prussia and Austria, a fight associated with the names of Frederick
the Great and the Empress Maria Theresa.

The Emperor Charles VI, head of the House of Habsburg, had no
son. Before he died he secured the support of the majority of the
important Powers of Europe for his plan, the Pragmatic Sanction,
as it was called. This provided that on his death his daughter Maria
Theresa should succeed to the Habsburg inheritance. Among those
who had given assent to the plan was Frederick William I, King of
Prussia and Elector of Brandenburg. In the same year, 1740, both

the Emperor Charles and King Frederick William died. To the throne of Prussia came a young prince, Frederick, later surnamed the Great, heir to a full state treasury and a well-trained and well-equipped army. "Ambition whispered to a listening ear" was his own later explanation of his actions. Completely disregarding his father's promise, he led his armies into the rich Austrian province of Silesia and seized it for the Prussian crown.

Thus in the very first year of his reign he had given proof of the military ability and the political ruthlessness which was to make him one of the most renowned monarchs of his time. Sixteen years later he was to have need of all his talents. For at the outbreak of the Seven Years War in 1756 Austria, France, Sweden, and Russia all combined to crush this upstart Power. Only Britain and Hanover were on his side. Frederick's military genius was of a high order, but in the end the combined weight of enemies became very dangerous. At the battle of Kunersdorf, east of Frankfurt-on-the-Oder, a combined Russian and Austrian army inflicted a severe defeat on the Prussians. Russian soldiers were deep in Germany, and even Berlin was threatened. Then, at the most critical moment for Frederick, fortune changed. His bitterest opponent, the Empress Elizabeth of Russia, died. She was succeeded by her nephew, Peter III, a devoted admirer of Frederick the Great. Peace followed and the danger was past. More was to come. The ancient kingdom of Poland had fallen into a state of political and administrative chaos and impotence. Russia and Prussia plotted to take advantage of the tempting opportunity. It will be remembered that the two historical component parts of the newly styled Kingdom of Prussia were, first, the old territory of the Teutonic Knights and, second, the lands of the Elector of Brandenburg. Between these two parts lay a large stretch of territory under the rule of Poland. In the year 1772 the First Partition of Poland took place. The Empress Maria Theresa had been persuaded by Russia and Prussia to join in the plan, though she repented of it, and, to her death, thought that she had betrayed the honour of her House and land by the robbery of

Polish territory. Indeed, the Partition was a cynical business. Russia took lands in White Russia, Austria took Galicia, and Frederick the Great added to his territory West Prussia, the Ermland, and the Netz district with the fortresses of Thorn and Bromberg.

Later hero-worshippers of Frederick the Great have tended to forget the decisive factor of the death of Elizabeth of Russia. Had this event not happened, the verdict of history on Frederick might well have been that he was a talented but reckless adventurer whose aggressive policy had concentrated enemies against his country and eventually brought it to ruin.

After the death of Frederick the state of Poland was twice more divided among its neighbours, till in the end it ceased to exist. These Second and Third Partitions of Poland took place, however, at a time when the outbreak of the French Revolution was already challenging the traditional shape of Europe. As a result of the Third Partition in 1795 the Prussian flag waved over the city of Warsaw, but this lasted but a few years—little longer, indeed, than the later eastward extension of German power created by the Treaty of Brest-Litovsk in 1918 or Hitler's ephemeral conquests in 1942. In the end it was Imperial Russia which profited most from the break-up of Poland. Prussia gained the district of Posen, and held it till the treaty of Versailles. But the Polish capital city, Warsaw, and a great area of the Vistula Valley remained a Russian province throughout the nineteenth century.

In 1703 British troops under John, Duke of Marlborough, had marched into Germany. In a series of wars over a span of one hundred and ten years the lands of Western Germany were a battlefield for British armies. That chapter of our military history was brought to an end in 1813. In an action at the village of Gorde, in Northern Hanover, the 73rd Foot, later known as the Second Battalion, The Black Watch, with half a rocket battery under the Hanoverian General Walmoden fought the French under Davoust. A few weeks later still, at the great battle of Leipzig, where for the first time almost all Germany combined against Napoleon, Britain was represented by a rocket battery, the Royal Horse Artillery. Not until the early weeks of 1945 did British units again fight on German soil.

This chapter has sketched briefly that period of the German story which spanned the gap between the medieval world and the world of modern history. Because of the destruction and chaos that followed the Thirty Years War it was specially fruitless and disappointing for Germany.

However, today it is possible to see four main factors of history in the middle of the eighteenth century which were to carry their influence into the following many years.

France and Britain were engaged in a century-long struggle which would in the end decide that British influence and not French would be dominant in the development of North America, India, and South Africa. That struggle had been, to some degree at least, fought out in Germany.

On the continent of Europe, France, under Louis XIII, Louis XIV and Louis XV, was the leading state, holding that position without serious challenge by virtue of her power, prestige, and culture. As the century neared its end serious internal tensions were manifest, but to the small principalities in Western Germany, the Court of Versailles remained the focal centre for all that was brilliant and socially desirable. For many years French influence was pre-eminent in German literature. Towards the end of the century, however, men like Lessing, Klopstock, Goethe, and others of the "German classics" established a native literature which broke away from the French tutelage.

The dynamic leadership of Frederick the Great had brought Prussia to a position where there was an open challenge to the traditional leadership of Habsburg Austria in Germany. A century was to elapse before the leadership was finally secured by Prussia. In the meantime there was a dualism in German politics which was a weakness. It would prove a deadly danger in the time of Napoleon Bonaparte.

69

A new great Power had appeared in the east. During the Northern War of 1719–21 Russian troops had appeared on the southern shores of the Baltic in battle against the Swedes. In the Seven Years War armies of the Empress Elizabeth of Russia had marched into the Neumark, the traditional territory of Brandenburg, and had threatened Berlin. The Partition of Poland brought some extension of territory to Prussia, but much more to Russia, and henceforward till 1919 there was to be no buffer state between the rulers at Berlin and St. Petersburg.

Thus was emphasized the open frontier to the east, a factor which was to exercise a powerful influence on Prussian and later on German thought. For between the German and the Slav peoples there was no mountain chain, no Pyreenees or Alps to form an obvious frontier or a natural defence. The frontier consisted of a line of border fortresses backed by an efficient and well-drilled army. Such a frontier environment fostered through the centuries a tough and militaristic frame of mind. Moreover, the frontier garrisons and the German squirearchy felt that they had behind them in the homeland orderly government, a settled state, and a tradition of learning and culture. In front of them, as they saw the picture, stretched a vast expanse of lightly developed countryside, peopled by a simple peasantry. Hence grew that significant difference between east and west in the German mind. There were quarrels in plenty between French and German, but the Rhinelanders and the people of South Germany have a proper respect for French culture and learning. Frederick the Great of Prussia was a great admirer of French ways. But towards the Slav feeling was different. There was a real fear of the Slav preponderance of numbers but no respect for their way of life. This despisal of the Slav peoples was to receive powerful impulse in the next century, when the Industrial Revolution converted Germany into a great and wealthy manufacturing state and left Russia in the relative condition of an agricultural community.

CHAPTER FIVE

NAPOLEON, BISMARCK, AND THE EMPEROR WILLIAM II (1789–1918)

AT the end of the eighteenth century the western part of the land of Germany was little more than a museum of antiquated political curiosities. Into that jumble of pocket-edition principalities, feudal bishoprics, and fossilized Free Cities the doctrines of the French Revolution and the armies of Napoleon were to come like the blast of a destroying tempest. Even in the first years of the Revolution the French General Custine, led his army into the Rhine Valley with his battlecry, "War to the tyrant's palace, peace to the poor man's cottage"—and found the countryside open to him. Without having to meet any real opposition he was able to occupy Speyer, Worms, and Mainz.

For the space of some dozen years Napoleon was to be master of Europe. That was partly due to his own great military ability, partly to the strength and resources of France, but partly also to the divisions among his opponents and to the inherent weakness of Germany. In the first year of the nineteenth century the doctrines of Liberty, Equality, and Brotherhood seemed to many Germans an improvement on the outworn feudalism of their local autocrats. It was only later, when French dominion became identified with the blockade of the coasts against English trade, or with the impressment of conscripts to fill Napoleon's armies, that a national German spirit of resistance emerged.

Even in the first days of the Revolution the cleft between Berlin and Vienna, which had begun with the Reformation and had been intensified under Frederick the Great, made itself obvious. In 1792 the armies of the Emperor and of the King of Prussia marched into France in defence of a threatened monarchical system. But the inconclusive cannonade of Valmy on September 20 was followed by the independent withdrawal of the two German forces, each anxious to cover its own most threatened territories. Disunity, in face of the threat from France, was carried much farther in 1795, when the King of Prussia made the Treaty of Basle with the French, whereby Prussia withdrew from the conflict on the promise that the French would not wage war north of a demarcation line which stretched from Mainz to Silesia.

So, while Prussia gained ten years of peace, Napoleon was able to carry his war into the Austrian Netherlands, into Italy, and across South Germany, until at the battle of Austerlitz, in Bohemia, in 1805 the Emperor of France, present in person, defeated the Emperors of Russia and of Austria. But little did Napoleon heed any demarcation line. As he felt the need to close the ports of the Continent to English shipping he moved on to the coast of Northern Germany. It was his willpower that was reorganizing the map of Germany. The Emperor Otto in the early Middle Ages had created prince-bishoprics as a balance weight to match the tribal dukedoms. Some of these had disappeared as a result of the Peace of Westphalia, but some still survived, especially along the Rhine Valley. Too small to be effective units in a modern world, they could not be merged by dynastic alliances nor managed into any secular confederation. Napoleon made short work of these anachronisms. Under his driving force a reorganization scheme was pushed through the Assembly of States. He created a Confederation of the Rhine, consisting, in essence, of the four states Bavaria, Baden, Wurttemberg, and Cassel—old-established German family domains but now greatly increased by the addition of territories allotted to them from former Church states and from the free cities. Thus Napoleon not only rationalized South Germany (to use a modern phrase), he also created a group of four states strongly bound to him by feelings of loyalty. To these he gave new ranks and dignities. It was, then, a French Emperor who elevated Bavaria and Wurttemberg to kingdoms and created the Grand Duchy of Baden. That fact showed how the Holy Roman Empire had already ceased to exist, even as a figment of man's imagination. The end came swiftly. On August 6, 1806, the Emperor Francis II of the House of Habsburg declared the Empire to be dissolved.

In Northern Germany Napoleon worked as drastically, though his methods were different. A great wedge of country, running right across the North German Plain, with its apex at Hamburg, was actually incorporated into the Territory of France. Napoleon meant to secure as firmly as possible his control of the coastline of the North Sea, essential to his policy of the blockade against British trade. So thoroughly was this plan carried into effect that in 1810 the city of Hamburg became a Department of France with a French administration. Farther south, in support, as it were, of this purely French seaboard, Napoleon organized the smaller units of Northwestern Germany into the Kingdom of Westphalia, under the rule of his brother, Jerome, and into the Grand Duchy of Berg.

When in 1806, too late for any effect, the King of Prussia declared war. Napoleon's answer was swift and decisive. In the double action of Jena and Auerstadt on October 14, 1806, the Prussian army was completely defeated. Of the tradition of Frederick the Great the drill and discipline had remained, but the leadership and tactics had become so formalized that they were no match for the new and supple fighting methods of the French.

From 1806 to 1812 Napoleon was master of all Germany up to the Elbe, and he controlled the policies of Prussia and Austria. Moreover, the French rule and influence in Western Germany was not that of a short-term military occupation. It had all the appearance of being there to stay. From Cassel, the capital of his kingdom in Westphalia, Jerome Bonaparte issued commissions written in French to the Hessian officers who served in his army, and appointed the selected few to be members of the Legion of Honour set up by his great brother.

Yet the very weight of this French control was invoking the almost inevitable reaction. There was a "German" spirit arising, born of a common resistance to the French. The King of Prussia at the time, Frederick William III, grandnephew to Frederick the Great, is no favourite of German historians. He was weak, hesitant, and was surrounded by a poor-spirited court. But his people, who had known a gleam of national spirit under the great Frederick in the middle of the century, were not content to be beaten at Jena and ordered about by Frenchmen. Led by a group of able and patriotic men, many of them not Prussian by birth—men like Von Stein, Scharnhorst, Von Gneisenau, and Blucher—a really national resistance movement arose.

Frederick William's Queen, Luise of Mecklenburg-Strelitz, a woman of courage and spirit, identified herself with the patriotic revival. A secret society, the "Tugenbund," spread the message of resistance to the invader. So, when the strength of the great French Emperor had been wasted in Russia, when the time for a war of liberation had clearly arrived, it was a wave of national enthusiasm among people and army which pushed a hesitant Prussian king into a position of leadership in the "Befreiungskrieg." Once the conflict started it was the Prussian soldiery who bore the brunt of the fighting, and in the end it was the Prussian Marshal Blucher who was the senior German general when the Allies entered Paris in 1815. To employ a phrase of admitted over-simplification, it was Prussia, rather than Austria, which had led the Germans against Napoleon.

The Congress of Vienna was an assembly of statesmen who sought to secure for Europe a period of established peace. In general they sought a return to formulae which had served well in the past. But even they were not going to attempt a return to the fragmentation of eighteenth-century Germany. Napoleon's reform and the decisions of the Congress reduced the three hundred and sixty units of adminstration to thirty-nine. Experience was soon to show that even these thirty-nine were far too many for the conditions of a modern age. It was, however, a gain that much of Napoleon's rationalization of the German map was allowed to remain. Prussia, as has been told, had led the war of freedom: Prussia, had, in the eyes of England and of other Powers at the Congress, a right to a good share in the redistributed Germany. One territory that was due for re-arrangement was the Napoleonic Kingdom of Westphalia. Part of that was made up of pieces of land long ago in the hands of Brandenburg—the bishoprics of Minden and Paderborn, and small parts of land on the Rhine. These were restored to Prussia, and with them went neighbouring lands on the Ruhr, the Lippe, and the Upper Ems. Included in these newly acquired lands was the ancient Free City of Essen. Like many other Imperial cities, it had lost its ancient privileges at the behest of Napoleon in 1802. It would not return to the status of a free city; it would become part of Prussia, and it would bring with it an asset which would become historical. For in 1810 one Friedrich Krupp had established an iron foundry in Essen.

Two matters of outstanding importance were veiled from the eyes of the diplomats of the Congress of Vienna. One was that the discovery of the steamboat and the steam locomotive were real events, destined to revolutionize transport. The other was that across the valleys of the Ruhr and the Emscher, now allocated by them to the Kingdom of Prussia, there stretched one of the great coalfields of the world. Within a few decades of the close of the Congress the King of Prussia was going to control, not only his Brandenburger Grenadiers and his Prussian General Staff, but also the industrial wealth of the Ruhr and the Rhineland and the wrought-iron cannon of the firm of Krupp.

Thus economic factors were to tilt the scales of Europe. To these were to be added social and biological factors. The rapidly increasing demands for industrial man-power for Westphalia and the Rhineland were largely met by the wholesale migration of the hardy peasant folk from the ancient Prussian lands. They moved from relatively serf-like conditions on the poor agricultural soil of Eastern Prussia into the well-paid industrial life of the towns, and there they raised large families. The population of Germany, as a whole, and of Prussia in particular, increased very rapidly during the middle of the last century. This was to have a notable effect on the balance of power not only in Germany but also in Europe. For three centuries or more the population of France had been substantially larger than that of any other European state. In days when the simple arithmetic of the counting of heads meant national greatness France was paramount. This situation was now to change. About the middle of the last century there were, for the first time, more Germans than Frenchmen in the world, and this disparity was destined to increase rapidly.

It was inevitable that the events of the Napoleonic period, the patriotic feelings aroused by the "Befreiungskrieg," the victories at Leipzig and Waterloo, the writings of Goethe and Schiller, all should combine to create the idea that, above Prussia, Bavaria, Baden, and the like, there was the greater conception of a Deutschland. To this conception there was now to be added an intensely practical argument. That thirty-nine states of various sizes and shapes scattered across Germany should, each and every one, have the right to Customs and Excise, that weights and measures should vary from state to state, that Hamburg should have its mark banco which was not current in Berlin—all this was clearly nonsense at a time when industrial revolution was bursting upon the world. It has been written that, more than anything else, it was the spread of the railway system that hastened the unification of Germany. When the first railway was built between Hamburg and Berlin it was necessary to negotiate a formal treaty among five, more or less independent, Powers. Obviously the chaos could not continue and a solution had to be found. But the search for the solution came up against great difficulty. There was to be a Deutschland. But what form should it take?

On August 26, 1841, Heinrich Hoffmann von Fallersleben, holidaying on the British island of Heligoland, wrote three verses which he obviously meant to be sung to an air by Haydn, already familiar as the tune of the Royal Hymn of the Austrian monarchy. He called his poem *Das Lied der Deutschen* (The Song of the Germans). The first line was "Deutschland, Deutschland uber alles" (Germany, Germany above everything)—this at a time when Germany as a political unit did not exist. Probably many readers now know that the war-time British idea that the words mean "Germany on top of everything" or "everybody" stems from a bad translation. At the same time it is perfectly true that Adolf Hitler did use the first verse of the song in a fashion not far removed from the worst British suspicions, and that by playing the tune always in association with his Horst-Wessel Lied he associated a fine old melody and reasonable words with his own tyrannical régime. For that reason the present German Government uses the third verse only of the original poem, "Einigkeit und Recht und Freiheit fur das deutsche Vaterland" (Unity and right and freedom for the German fatherland), of course to the Haydn melody.

The Deutschland which von Fallersleben and other thinkers and patriots, young and old, were seeking could take one of two forms —a "Grossdeutschland" or a "Kleindeutschland," a great Germany or a small Germany—and the difference turned on the position of Austria. The "Grossdeutschland" meant that Austria would be within the future state, would presumably lead the future state. But what then would be the position of the great non-German portions of the Austro-Hungarian Empire, the Magyars, the Czechs, the Italians, the Slovenes, and the Croats? Were they to be within or without the new state? "Kleindeutschland" meant a Germany without Austria. That meant, without any doubt, a domination by Prussia. Such a solution was not going to be particularly popular in South Germany, in Bavaria, and the other kingdoms. In the three Hanseatic Free Cities of Bremen, Hamburg, and Lubeck opinion was strongly divided. Prussia was tough, hustling, rather uncultured, wanting her own way, and a bit rough in her methods.

77

In practice, the situation was going to be complicated by the fact that there were other thoughts which were also engaging the minds of men of vision and energy, thoughts of democratic government and of liberal reform. Since the end of the Thirty Years War autocracy had been enthroned in Germany. The armies of Napoleon had, it is true, brought with them the revolutionary idea of France, but the defeat of Napoleon had been followed by a wave of reaction. The great majority of the princes who ruled the German states, such as they existed after the Congress of Vienna, were men firmly opposed to any infringement of their personal rule. The "July Revolution" of 1830 in France had been followed by other revolutionary movements in many countries of Europe and in most states in Germany. Princes, under pressure from the people, had promised liberal constitutions, freedom of the Press, and so on. Then there had come, once again, reaction. Once more the lead had come from Paris. On February 23, 1848, the population of Paris rose against King Louis Philippe and drove him from France. All over Europe the forces of reform were encouraged and stirred again.

It was on May 18 of that year, 1848, that some five hundred notable Germans, delegates from all the states of the German Bund—Austria was, of course, included—met with great ceremony in the St. Paul's Church at Frankfurt-on-Main, to constitute themselves a German National Assembly. They were filled with enthusiasm for the Germany of their dreams. Yet the Conference was a failure, partly, perhaps, because two aims were confused and impeded one another. These were the desire for German unity and the liberal urge for democratic institutions. In the face of Austrian resistance and without any clear lead from Prussia, the Conference broke up in despair.

One result of this blow to liberal thought was the emigration of tens of thousands of Germans who despaired of being able to find free institutions in their own country. Throughout the nineteenth century this tide of German emigration went on, bringing hard-working and intelligent settlers to the United States, Canada, Brazil, the Argentine, and elsewhere.

However, among those who had been present at the meetings in the St. Paul's Church was a Prussian official named Otto von Bismarck. He made up his mind that the solution of the problem of German unity was to be in the form of the "Kleindeutschland," a new Germany under Prussian leadership. This idea was partly based on the belief that Prussia was better suited than Austria to lead a new Germany. The economic importance of the Ruhr was already manifest, and the Ruhr was in Prussian hands. Yet the line of thought which carried most weight with Bismarck was the question of the future of the non-German parts of the Austrian Empire. If Austria came into the Germany of the future, then, as he saw it, the non-German parts would most certainly fall away, and there was only one direction in which they could fall—into the lap of Russia. A Russian garrison in Bohemia, due south of Berlin, was what Bismarck was determined at almost any cost to avoid. In his view Bohemia was to be neither German nor Russian. Therefore it must remain Austrian. Therefore the Austrian Empire in its existing form must be preserved, though it meant pushing Austria outside the new Germany. Later generations have indeed seen the break-up of the Austro-Hungarian Empire and a Bohemia which is a satellite state of Russia.

At least one complication had been removed. In 1837 the personal union between Great Britain and Hanover came to an end. The Salic law applied in Hanover but not in Westminster. So Victoria became Queen, and her uncle Ernest, Duke of Cumberland, became King Ernst August of Hanover. It would have made Bismarck's task very difficult if the Duke of Kent had had a son instead of a daughter.

In 1862 Bismarck, at the age of forty-seven, became Prussian Prime Minister and Minister for Foreign Affairs. He had already decided on his policy. He would have to overcome great hesitation on the part of his royal master, but he had the instruments of his plan ready to his hand—Von Moltke for his Commander-in-Chief, the Prussian General Staff, the needle-gun for his infantry, the Krupp breech-loaders for his artillery, and the railways and telegraphs of the Prussian State system with which to move and control his armies. It was the essence of Bismarck's political strategy that he knew how to exasperate his opponents into making the false step and that he knew how to control his own king and generals when victory was assured. Bismarck stands out as the genius of the limited objective. In 1864 he accepted a war alongside Austria against Denmark, over the question of Schleswig and Holstein. That was soon over and the limited objective achieved. The two duchies came under combined Austrian-Prussian control; no further action was taken against Denmark. By 1866 he had so annoyed Austria that the Emperor actually declared war on Prussia and summoned the German princes to his aid. Bismarck was ready for this, and it did not add to his worries that, with no great enthusiasm, the armies of Hanover, Saxony, and Bavaria marched towards a hoped-for junction with Austrian forces. At Langensalza, in Thuringia, the Prussians under General Vogel von Falkenstein defeated, without great loss on either side, the ill-equipped forces of Hanover. On July 3, at Koniggratz, in North-eastern Bohemia, the white-clad infantry of the Habsburgs went into action armed with muzzle-loaders. as they had done so often and with such gallantry, during centuries of warfare. But they were fighting not only Prussian infantry, good soldiers with a breech-loading rifle; they were fighting a modern industrial state, whole armies were concentrated on to the field of action by railway and by telegraph from head-quarters in Berlin. The defeat of the Austrian army was absolute, and nothing lay in the way of a triumphant Prussian march to Vienna save the strong mind of one man—Bismarck. It took a very painful scene with his own royal master and plenty of arguments with the generals before he was able to achieve his main idea. Austria was to be cleared out of the way but by no means crushed or humiliated, not to be turned into an implacable foe. In the same way, though Hanover was annexed to Prussia, the two other German states, Saxony and Bavaria were not to be humbled. The sound wisdom of his policy was to be seen four years later. This time it was Napoleon III, Emperor of France, who had been manoeuvred into making the false move. It was a French declaration of war against the North German Confederation on July 19, 1870, which opened the way for Bismarck's final victory in strategic diplomacy. Because he had used moderation after his previous victories, Austria did not move in aid of France, and the South German Kings and Grand Dukes sent their armies to join those of North Germany in the advance on Paris. The Prussian army was strong, well armed, and well led. The French armies had gallantry and not much else. Now Bismarck had the greatest of all allies on the side of his plan for the future—the irrefutable arguments of plain facts. The armies of a united Germany, led by the kings and princes in uniform, were assembled as victors in the heart of France. The idea that this union in war should take permanent form was so clamant that not the hesitancy of the King of Prussia, not the jealousies of the King of Bavaria, could stand in the way. On January 18, 1871, in the Hall of Mirrors in the Palace of Versailles, King William of Prussia was acclaimed "Deutscher Kaiser"—German Emperor.

It is interesting to remember that the impressive ceremony in the Hall of Mirrors closed with the playing of the Prussian national hymn Heil Dir im Siegeskranz to Henry Carey's melody which we know as God Save the Queen. The flag of the new Empire was that black, white, and red flag of horizontal stripes which had come into existence, three years previously, as the flag of the North German Confederation. Black and white were the colours of Prussia, and red and white were the colours of the Hanse cities. The new flag, therefore, did in fact emphasize the predominantly North German influence in the new Empire.

What had been thus achieved was not an ideal solution. It was hurried and patched together, born of the necessities of the industrial revolution and the war against France. It was a league of princes,

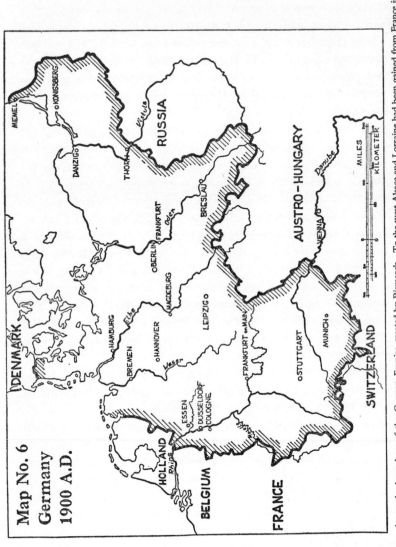

Map No. 6
Germany
1900 A.D.

This map shows the boundary of the German Empire created by Bismarck. To the west Alsace and Lorraine had been gained from France in 1871. To the north Schleswig and Holstein had been incorporated in Prussia in 1866. To the east the ancient kingdom of Poland had disappeared and there was a common frontier between Germany and Russia.

and many of them thought, with a good deal of justice, that Bismarck had jockeyed them into doing something they did not entirely desire. What he thought can be judged by a remark of his made some four years earlier. "Arbeiten wir rasch. Heben wir Deutschland sozusagen in den Sattel. Reiten wird es schon konnen." (Let's get to work. Let us heave Germany into the saddle. She will soon learn to ride.)

The new state faced a number of unsolved problems inside the body politic which older countries had worked out over a period of years. Bismarck had no great respect for parliamentary government and did not like socialism. He wanted a strong central government exercised in the name of his monarch. However, his foreign policy was cautious and realistic. He wished to support Austria, now that she was no longer a danger to his policy for Germany. He wished to pursue a policy of conciliation towards France and was against the annexation of the whole of Alsace and Lorraine to Germany. He thought that only those parts which were linguistically akin to German should be taken from France. In this view he was overruled. He wished for friendship with England. Towards Russia he was cautious. His view was that, as he said, Germany was a saturated land, a land which had now reached its natural boundaries. The danger of his policy lay in the fact that, in the pursuit of what he thought to be good for his country, he had stifled opposition and had built up a constitutional machine which depended upon the power and prestige of the monarch. That served him well enough while the monarch was the old King he had known for so many years. But in the one year of 1888 Germany had three Emperors. The old Kaiser Wilhelm I died on March 9. His son, the distinguished army commander of the French war, liberal-minded, a friend to England, married to the daughter of Queen Victoria, ascended the throne as the Emperor Frederick III, knowing that his days were already numbered. He died, on June 15, of cancer. Within three months the crown of Germany passed from an emperor ninety-two years old to a prince of twenty-nine.

This young man of twenty-nine, Kaiser Wilhelm II, had succeeded to a great inheritance. Expressed in terms of size alone, his Germany was more than twice the size of Great Britain. From Mulhouse, in Alsace, to Memel, on the Baltic, was a distance of 830 miles. The population had already reached forty-nine million and was obviously, on the basis of all known statistics, to continue to rise at a rapid rate. Steel and iron production were increasing, increasing so fast that it appeared probable that before long they would overtop the production of Great Britain, at that time the great manufacturing centre of the world. A German overseas empire was coming into being. At first Bismarck had little enthusiasm for territories in tropical Africa. He had said that Germany was a satisfied land. However, in the latter days of his Chancellorship he agreed to give his support to overseas expansion, and it was under his encouragement that Germany acquired possessions in West and South-west Africa, in East Africa, and in New Guinea. Hamburg merchants had established trading stations in the Cameroons and Zanzibar early in the century and these warehouses and offices were under the flag of Hamburg. Their enterprise thus made it possible for Germany to take part in that scramble for African territory indulged in by most of the great Powers towards the latter half of the nineteenth century. As an outlet for German trade and as a home for German emigrants these possessions were only of limited value. Nevertheless, they satisfied prestige requirements, and Germany felt that she was becoming one of the world colonial Powers. Contemplating Germany as she was at the end of the century it is obvious to present-day observers that the one great requirement for her solid success would have been calm and steady internal development coupled with a foreign policy which eschewed adventure. But the new Emperor was restless, ambitious, and vain. Some who knew him judged him to be pathologically unstable. From his birth his right arm had been withered and useless. This defect preyed on his mind. It was probably the reaction against physical deficiency which led him to be theatrical and self-assertive in later years. Between such a man and the old Chancellor co-operation was certain to be difficult; as it happened the end came quite quickly. In 1890 the Emperor dismissed his grandfather's faithful servant. The cartoon "Dropping the Pilot" by Tenniel which appeared in *Punch* has become one of the great political cartoons of history.

Families who gain riches quickly are often uncomfortable neighbours. The Germans had gained wealth and power in one short half-century. So far as it is possible to generalize about a people, it is reasonable comment to say that the Germans lack patience and a sense of proportion. They are carried away by their emotions. The Emperor William II possessed these German failings in an exaggerated form. He was dazzled and thrown off his balance by the apparent strength of his country. Thanks to the coal of the Ruhr and the iron of Lorraine, thanks to the inventiveness of her chemists and the skilled workmanship of her people, she was on the way to becoming the world's greatest industrial Power. The German people were virile, youthful, and fertile. All these signs of national greatness fostered the vanity of a young monarch already all too inclined to the role of an Emperor. He lacked the common sense to see that even the German Emperor could not afford to make enemies on every hand. So the world had to witness one impulsive action after another. When in 1895 Dr. Jameson led a raid into the Transvaal Republic in an attempt to upset the Boer Government of President Kruger, William II sent a telegram of congratulation to Kruger on the defeat of the raiders. This did the Boers no good and caused much ill-feeling in England. The Emperor's desire to be in the limelight led to speech-making which was often rash and exaggerated in form. There was grandiloquent phrases about "shining armour" and "our future lies upon the water." In the same spirit of careless confidence the "Ruckversicherungsvertrag," the treaty of reinsurance with Russia, upon which Bismarck had laid such weight, was allowed to lapse and was not renewed.

Because German unity had been achieved late in history the

German race had not been able to play its part in the great days of colonial expansion, when Spain and Portugal, France, Holland, and England were building up wide overseas empires. This was exasperating to the Emperor and, indeed, to many Germans, who felt that fate had dealt harshly with a great people.

Some of the Kaiser's most flamboyant indiscretions were due to the influence of a number of pressure groups, the Colonial League, the German Naval League, and, above all, that of Grand Admiral von Tirpitz and his friends. In North Africa and in the Mediterranean he had angered France and Russia. The Emperor now proceeded to make an enemy of Great Britain. Bismarck was prepared to have overseas colonies but not to build a fleet for their protection. William II now announced his intention of building a fleet, a definite challenge to the British command of the sea. Already Europe had commenced to align itself into two camps. France and Russia had a military agreement; Germany, Austria, and Italy had a form of triple alliance. To press Great Britain into military discussions with France was the height of the Emperor's folly.

By 1910 the Kaiser's diplomacy had achieved the fateful result that his country had only one friend in the world; that friend was Austria. Germany's isolation was so complete that she was now diplomatically dependent on the ramshackle Empire of the Dual Monarchy to the south. How long this Empire could hold itself together was questionable. The various non-German peoples of the Empire were openly hostile to the powerful Austrian element which, in their view, controlled the capital city and its ministries. The old Emperor, Franz Josef II, was rapidly losing his grip of affairs; his heir, the Archduke Ferdinand, was a man who might have saved the situation through his knowledge of the Slav problem and his personal prestige among the non-German parts of the Empire. On June 28, 1914, the Archduke Ferdinand and his wife were shot in the narrow streets of Sarajevo, in Bosnia. There was remote evidence that the assassination had been planned from Serbia. Conrad von Hotzendorf, the Austrian Chief of the General Staff, had made up his mind that, unless Pan-Slav aspirations could receive a blow through the extinction of Serbia, the Austro-Hungarian Empire was, in any event, doomed. The Austrian Foreign Ministry thought that a cheap victory of Serbia would be worth having. Remotely they realized that Russia might intervene to protect the southern Slavs. Vaguely they hoped that German support for Austrian policy would deter Russia from intervening militarily on the side of the Serbs.

For years the planning sections of all the general staffs of Europe had reckoned in terms of some great "Battle of the Frontiers" which would bring military victory—or defeat—within a period of six weeks. There had been a book, *The Great Illusion* which had considerable influence on informed thought, but not in the way that the author had intended. Norman Angell had set out to prove that great wars were no longer possible because the disruption of financial and economic life would impose an intolerable burden upon the fighting nations. Some, however, had read his lesson to mean that war must be short. The logical conclusion was that everything must be keyed to obtain a swift military success. Yet in their planning the German generals were confronted by the defects of the Kaiser's adventurous and hazardous foreign policy. Germany and Austria were allies. So, nominally, was Italy a member of the Triple Alliance but her enthusiasm had worn thin. By 1914 it seemed likely that Italy would not automatically, by virtue of a treaty, fight alongside Germany and Austria. Indeed her neutrality was so nearly certain that France would not need to maintain fighting formations on the Italian frontier. England had negotiated an *Entente Cordiale* with France in 1904. This had gone a considerable distance towards a satisfactory settlement of various matters which had, in the past, caused friction between the two nations. In January 1906 just after a General Election in England had returned a Liberal Government under Sir Henry Campbell-Bannerman to Westminster with a large majority, Mr. Haldane, the Secretary of State for War was authorized by his Prime Minister to initiate technical discussions at staff level to co-ordinate British and French military operations in certain eventualities. The main outcome of these discussions was within Britain itself, the formation under Mr. Haldane's aegis of the British Expeditionary Force of six divisions. Yet it was made clear to France that eventual British action would have to be decided by the Cabinet of the day.

The German General Staff were faced with the problem which Bismarck had sought to avoid, the prospect of a war on two fronts. If the reactions and the military value of Italy and Great Britain were not certain, they had two grim and momentous certainties on which to reckon. In combination France and Russia could produce in the field armies far larger than those of Germany, or even Germany and Austria acting together. In Russia distances were great and mobilization would be slow. Therefore, so they argued, a decisive blow must be delivered against France, a blow of such shattering force that any fighting recovery would be impossible. Thereafter the bulk of the German armies could be transferred to the eastern front to join the armies of Austria-Hungary in a war against Tzarist Russia. On the narrow front common to France and Germany manoeuvre was impossible. Therefore a Chief of the German General Staff, Count von Schlieffen, devised the plan which bears his name. This involved the march of four great German armies across Belgian soil, in order to carry out a massive outflanking movement with the German right wing. As the great swing took place the main French armies were to be pinned to the ground by German attacks so that eventually the whole fighting forces of France were to be driven up against their eastern fortresses and the annihilating victory achieved.

As tension grew in July 1914 there were few Governments or War Ministries which could force themselves to think of a war which might last for years. So obsessed were the generals with the need to have their own armies immediately ready in battle array that they were not ready to grant to the diplomats even one or two days wherein to attempt to avert a threatening wholesale catas-

88

trophe. Germany had given a pledge of support to her only remaining ally and could not now withdraw it for fear of a great diplomatic defeat. Therefore, impelled by fear, the fear of foreign armies marching across their frontiers, the great Powers of Europe, one by one sent the orders for mobilization which were to commence the First World War. First Austria ordered mobilization against Serbia, then on the 28th declared war. Then followed the relentless strokes of fate in days when few men took pause to ask whither they were going. Russia mobilized against Austria. Austria ordered general mobilization. France followed suit, so did Russia, so did Germany. On August 1 Germany declared war against Russia, on the 2nd against France. That same day Germany's representative in Brussels declared his country's intention to march through Belgian territory and demanded free passage. King Albert of Belgium appealed to the British Government. The Cabinet of the Liberal Prime Minister, Mr. Asquith, was well nigh unanimous in its decision. The British ambassador in Berlin was instructed to say that, unless the German Government stopped any forward movement through Belgian land, Great Britain would consider herself at war with Germany. The Schlieffen Plan had history within its grip. England and Germany were at war. It was midnight of August 3.

Already, on August 1 the immense machine of mobilization had commenced to work. Eight great German armies, one and a half million men, commenced to form up along the western frontiers of Germany, ready to move forward into Belgium and France. It was Bismarck's Germany in battle array, for the Third Army was Saxon, commanded by General von Hausen, formerly the Saxon Minister for War, the Fourth Army was under the Crown Prince of Wurttenberg. The sixth Army was Bavarian, its commander Prince Rupprecht, Crown Prince of Bavaria. The whole host moved under the supreme command of the German Emperor. For the first time the soldiery discarded their blue and wore the new field grey uniforms issued to them at mobilization centres. As an operation of co-ordinated staff work it was masterly.

As a piece of statecraft it was hazardous in the extreme. The influence of the General Staff on the Kaiser and indeed on the German people was very great. It would have seemed treasonable to suggest that the Schlieffen Plan might fail. And if it did fail what then? England had been brought in. Militarily her contribution might not be important at first, but her potential strength was great. Yet if the Plan gave to Germany overwhelming victory in the west within the first six weeks of the conflict, England's potential could be discounted. The march across Belgium did violate a treaty, but after swift victory Belgium could be placated and some compensation paid. So the advocates of the Plan would have argued.

Everything depended upon the timetable success of the Plan and diplomacy had been subordinated to marching troops. Yet, even on military grounds the Schlieffen Plan was, in 1914, already out of date. Seen from this distance of time it can only appear as an unjustifiable hazard. The German superiority in numbers on the Western Front was not overwhelming. There was no factor of safety to cover unpredictable developments. Had the tactical training in the French army been better, had the French infantry been taught the use of field entrenchments and the stopping power of modern firearms then the German armies might well have been held on the frontier. As it was, French errors in tactics and generalship allowed the German armies to reach and cross the Marne. But General Joffre did not lose his nerve, the regrouping of the French forces was a brilliant piece of improvization, in the open country of Champagne the French 75 mm. field gun dominated the battle. General von Moltke from his supreme headquarters of the German Army at Spa in Luxembourg was out of touch with the course of the great battle. The German armies were halted and must withdraw. The Schlieffen Plan had failed. Its basic design was the defeat of the French armies in the first six weeks of the war. The French armies were not defeated. They had suffered severe losses through their own bravery and poor tactical teaching, but they were intact.

The war was to last for four more years but its history would be dominated by the failure of Schlieffen's great plan and what came after.

In the months of the Battle of the Marne large Austro-Hungarian armies had advanced into Russian Poland and there they had been defeated. Two Russian armies, moving with disastrous lack of co-ordination, had penetrated into East Prussia. The decisive victory over the Russians at Tannenberg gave to the German people an epic memory to cheer them in dark days and the name of the two commanders Hindenburg and Ludendorff. Yet huge Russian forces, not yet committed to battle, were massing. In the west the prerequisite victory had not been achieved by Germany, in the East the situation was threatening and demanded urgent action. Nevertheless her armies were in occupation of nearly all Belgium and of ten departments of France, including the coalmining areas of the north. This fact was to dominate the entire war. The Western Allies were constrained to a policy of constant attacks, attempts to reduce the German hold on French and Belgian soil. They had also, so far as was possible, to weaken the force of the Central Powers assault on Russia.

The strain of the vast operation of invasion and the disappointment of the Marne had taken heavy toll on the health of the Chief of the German General Staff, Helmuth von Moltke. He resigned his post and was succeeded by General von Falkenhayn. There was one more attempt to regain for Germany the initiative in the west. Both sides had prolonged their northern flank in the so-called "race to the sea." Both sides were beginning to realize that, in Flanders as in Picardy, once well trained, tough, fighting infantry had secured hold on a village they could only be dislodged by assembling a really heavy concentration of artillery fire. What such fire could do against small targets had already been shown at Liège and Maubeuge and was to be seen at Antwerp. There the forts were crushed under the fire of sixteen-inch mortars from German coast artillery and twelve-inch mortars brought from the Austrian siege train. But the Belgian Army withdrew and held the coast.

Germany had, by a great effort of improvization, created four completely new army corps composed of volunteers from university students and other categories not called up in the first mobilization. In October von Falkenhayn sent these new formations, the XXII, XXIII, XXV and XXVII Reserve Corps, to the Belgian front and launched them against the Allied lines between Dixmude and Messines. The attacks were made with fantastic bravery and a complete disregard of the lessons of the fighting of the Marne. The advancing ranks of young Germany dissolved under the fire of French "seventy-fives" and British eighteen-pounder guns. Only a mile or so of territory was gained at a price of terrible losses. The assault at Langemarck was a tragedy remembered in Germany for many a long year. The total failure of the offensive of these four reserve corps, associated in British minds with the First Battle of Ypres, was the last German attempt to secure a decision in the west until Ludendorff's great spring offensive of 1918. The War of Position had begun.

Thereafter the German trench system through France and Belgium assumed the form of a great fortress which the powers of the Entente felt bound to attack. It was long before the generals, or the troops, on either side realized the implications of this gigantic operation of siege warfare. For the Allies it was to mean the costly battles of Artois and Champagne, of Verdun and the Somme. Then came the tragic failure of the Nivelle offensive of 1917 and the engagement of the British Army in the battle in the mud of Flanders before Ypres. While all this was happening in the west, wars of movement on a huge scale were being waged upon other fronts. Turkey entered the war on the side of the Central Powers, Italy on the side of the Entente. Russian armies penetrated deep into Austro-Hungary, German armies into Russia. Nations and peoples were becoming war weary. Russia was tiring, Austria was tiring, so was Italy.

On April 6, 1917, a new and powerful force entered upon the scene. The United States of America declared war on Germany.

Yet, for a time, this reinforcement for the Entente might seem, to the German people to be more than balanced by the collapse of Russia. To them the war had brought notable victories but also hardship and privations. There were those who thought that the disappearance of Russia from the conflict might give an opportunity for a negotiated peace. The Socialists in the Reichstag introduced a motion calling upon the Government to initiate discussions upon possible terms for peace. There were mutinies in the German fleet at Kiel. The Kaiser was forced to change his Chancellor and his Chief of Staff. Hindenburg and Ludendorff were called to take command of all German forces. Under their leadership plans were made for the continuance of the war and for victory in 1918.

All through the winter of 1917–18 divisions released from the eastern theatre of war by the collapse of Russia were brought by train across Germany, refitted and trained for a last and final offensive in the west which should bring victory. The background resembled the problem which confronted von Schlieffen so many years earlier. Complete victory must be obtained quickly. The increasing strength of the American armies in France was a portent of threatening disaster to Germany. It was becoming all too evident that German submarines could not check the arrival of these reinforcements. As Ludendorff saw his problem he must risk everything to secure a crushing military victory, not by an outflanking movement as in 1914, but by a violent thrust at the point of junction of the French and British armies. Yet, as in 1914, it was wildy hazardous. There was no margin of safety, no alternative plan should the great gamble fail. Yet, for the people of Germany, the possibility of failure was not to be contemplated.

At first the news which came from the Western Front was splendid. The German divisions had broken through the thinly held front of General Gough's Fifth Army and seemed on the point of driving the British to the sea. A further attack, more to the south, brought the Germans to within fifty miles of Paris. A giant cannon commenced to shell the French capital. The news and the pictures in the newspapers of Berlin and other German cities were exhilarating. All appeared hopeful until that fateful day of July 17 when a combined French and American army under the supreme direction of Marshal Foch attacked out of the forest of Villers Cotteret against the exposed flank of the deepest enemy salient. Three weeks later there came even more alarming news. On August 8, 1918, the British Army under command of Sir Douglas Haig assumed the offensive and in a massive assault of tanks and infantry overran in one day the German positions in front of Arras. Six days later, in a conference held before the Kaiser at general headquarters at Spa in Luxembourg, Ludendorff told his astonished hearers that the military war had been lost and that an armistice must be obtained as rapidly as possible.

The full seriousness of the position was not realized by his fellow countrymen. German troops were still deep in France and Belgium. The German Army had once before recovered from an Allied counter-attack on the Marne in 1914 and there seemed now to be no obvious reason why a fighting withdrawal should not be carried out to some strong defensive line, on whose firm basis negotiations for a peace settlement might be commenced. Ludendorff himself knew that this was an unrealistic hope. Yet, in fact, the German withdrawal was achieved in good order. The Allied pursuit was hampered by destroyed roads and autumn mud and, as the decisive date for the Armistice negotiations drew near it might have seemed to German soldiers and people alike that all was not lost. The true position was very different. On the southern sector of the Western Front Marshal Foch was massing half a million men for his proposed Lorraine offensive. The Army Group "de Castelnau," composed of the 10th French Army under General Mangin, the 8th French Army under General Gerrard and the 2nd United States Army under General Bullard, were soon to be set in motion in a great operation which, striking through Metz, was planned to reach the Rhine and cut off the German armies retreating in Belgium.

That offensive was never launched. Marshal Foch decided that the casualties which would inevitably be suffered by France would not justify the political advantages of a great final military victory.

Certainly no historian has a right to judge whether the Marshal's, decision in this regard was correct or otherwise. It is, however, true that the absence of a final advance of victorious Allied armies on to German soil and a German defeat in the field did open the way to the seductive legend among some Germans of the "stab in the back." For while the German armies in France and Belgium were slowly withdrawing, almost out of touch with pursuers, able to maintain an intact front, a mutiny had broken out among naval units at Kiel. This was followed by riots and unrest in Berlin, Munich and other cities. There were heated scenes in the Reichstag. Extreme left-wing leaders attempted to seize control. It was in the afternoon of November 9 that a group of Socialists, Ebert and Scheidermann at their head, declared themselves the leaders of the German Republic. The Kaiser abdicated and withdrew to Holland. On November 11 the Armistice was signed.

CHAPTER SIX

THE WEIMAR REPUBLIC AND HITLER
(1918–45)

THE Great War was ended on November 11, 1918. It had commenced in the guise of a punitive expedition of Austrian troops against Serbia. It had lasted for four and a half years and had caused casualties and expenditure of treasure on an unprecedented scale. Three traditional empires, Russia, Austria and Germany had crashed in ruins. To set the world on a secure path of peace would demand wisdom and statecraft of a high order. The times were not propitious for calm thinking. Even among the victorious Allies the war had ended in an atmosphere of disillusionment. Italy, oppressed with the memories of her defeat by the Austrians and Germans at Caporetto and with a completely disorganized economy, was very near civil war. France, saddened by the terrible losses in long years of fighting, oppressed with the memories of the failure of the Nivelle offensive of 1917, was bitter and cynical. Even for relatively powerful England the years of war had brought disappointment. The millions of civilian soldiery called to the fight as volunteers or as conscripts, had grown suspicious of their military leadership. The casualties on the Somme, at Paschendaele, on Gallipoli or in Mesopotamia had seemed to be disproportionate to the results obtained. It was popular gossip that the Prime Minister, Mr. Lloyd George, was out of sympathy with his military commanders. Of all the Allied Powers only the United States, which had come late into the war, remained in 1918 relatively fresh with her military potential still undeployed. The President, Mr. Woodrow Wilson, had gained for himself a high esteem in Europe, not entirely matched by his position in his own country, where he had failed to secure the agreement of the Republican Senators in his plans for world peacemaking.

In order that the war might be fought Great Britain had spent or had pledged the great wealth of her overseas capital and credit. She had made heavy cash advances to France and had in turn borrowed largely from the United States. Perhaps by reason of mental weariness the statesmen of that period were not able to comprehend what had been the impact of the Great War on world economy. In the British General Election of 1918 Mr. Lloyd George had used the slogans "Hang the Kaiser" and "Make Germany Pay." There were few economists calm enough to see clearly that payment could only be made by the transfer of gold, whereof there is only a limited supply in the whole world, or by the transfer of capital equipment or by the creation of exports. In England, in the years 1919 and 1920 the public mind was bemused by industrial unrest and strikes and facile catchwords "Homes fit for heroes" and "a brave new world."

The two leaders of the Entente M. Georges Clemenceau and Mr. Lloyd George had been at the head of their respective governments at the time of gravest danger in 1918. It was but human that they should see themselves as victors disposing of a defeated Germany. Mr. Wilson's ideals were lofty but some of his plans were doctrinaire and his economic theses were not always sound. On the German side Ebert and Noske, the civilian Minister for War, were men of great courage and ability, but they suffered terribly in the eyes of many fellow countrymen from the fact that they belonged to that Socialist party which had, in 1917, proposed the resolution in the Reichstag in favour of a negotiated peace. In the minds of many, perhaps of the majority of the ex-soldiers from the Western Front, they would always be associated with the untrue legend of "stab in the back."

The Treaty of Versailles laid down the terms for peace. The two provinces of Alsace and Lorraine were to be restored to France. In the north a plebiscite was to be held in Schleswig to decide what portion of that province should return to Denmark. The ancient kingdom of Poland was to be reconstituted by the return of lands which had been held by Russia, Austria and Germany. The result, so far as Germany was concerned was that Poland regained almost all the territory that had been lost to Prussia in the days of Frederick the Great. There was some attempt to delininate frontiers according to ethnological factors but this was difficult. There had been much movement of population in the course of a century and a half and there was bound to be some hardship.

The Treaty decided that those overseas possessions which had been German colonies should be put under the trusteeship of the League of Nations. It was in the clauses dealing with reparations that the gravest miscalculations were made.

The war had brought great destruction, and German armies had occupied large areas of France and Belgium. The basic idea of the Treaty, powerfully supported by the French Premier, Clemenceau, was that Germany was responsible for everything and Germany should make good. "The economic clauses of the Treaty were malignant and silly to the extent which made them obviously futile." That is a quotation from the first volume of Winston Churchill's memoirs. Article 231 of the Versailles Treaty, the famous war-guilt clause, forced the German delegates to admit that Germany was alone responsible for the war. British thought on the subject of responsibility tended to be influenced by the German invasion of Belgium. German thought was much more mixed. Men of high moral standards would have accepted much responsibility, but they would have said that Austria and Russia also carried their share of the blame. Faced with the impossibility of an effective resistance, the German post-war Government, consisting of Majority Socialists, Centre Party, and Democrats, men who represented the old Socialist, Catholic, and liberal traditions, some of them men who had in their youthful days fought against militarism, accepted the Treaty with its war-guilt clause, and thus more than ever rendered the Government of Germany obnoxious to many of their fellow-countrymen.

The Constitution of the new Germany was worked out at an assembly held in the small Thuringian town of Weimar. This relatively quiet location was intentionally chosen to remove the deliberations from the heated atmosphere of great cities. The Constitution was based on an extreme form of proportional representation; it was intended to be fair to every shade of opinion. In fact, it encouraged the growth of small parties representing local or particularist views. Morover, insasmuch as voting was on party lists, it took away the feeling of the responsibility of the parliamentary candidate to any definite city or countryside. The Weimar Constitution was a constitution which raised the party system to heights of exaggerated importance. To emphasize the break with the past the black, white, and red flag of the Kaiser's Empire was abolished. In its place the Weimar Republic adopted the black, red, and gold flag, the colours of the 1848 assembly at Frankfurt-on-Main, the colours also of the medieval Empire.

One of the features of the war had been the rapid extension of the German Army, bringing with it very heavy demands for additional officers. The regular officer corps, even the first echelon of Reserve Officers, were by no means able to meet the need, and many men had been commissioned as reserve officers with little previous training and with few family or educational traditions to fit them for the post. These men, many of them in their early twenties, with four and a half years of war behind them, with no civilian training, no civilian employment in sight, and memories only of an officer's position in battle, became a real danger. Defeated Germany was faced with industrial chaos and much unemployment. It was such types who banded themselves together into the Freikorps and fought the Poles in Upper Silesia. It was they who organized the right-wing Kapp Putsch and tried to seize power in Berlin. It was precisely these people who formed the first group around Adolf Hitler.

Adolf Hitler was born in Austria, it is suggested of mixed Austrian and Czech blood. His family life had been miserable; he had been unhappy before the war in Vienna, slightly happier in Munich, and, because he disliked Austria and liked Bavaria, he had obtained special permission, as an Austrian subject, to enlist as a soldier in the army of the King of Bavaria. He was employed as a battalion runner, and rose to the rank of corporal. He was badly wounded on the British front in 1916. After convalescing he returned to his unit, and was temporarily blinded in a 1918 gas attack. Although the story of his Iron Cross Class I is somewhat wrapped in mystery, it may well be that it was a decoration genuinely won. If so, he must have shown considerable bravery, for the Iron Cross Class I was very rarely given to the junior rank of corporal. In hospital, recovering from mustard-gas blindness, he heard the news of the collapse of Germany. Hitler was a man whose whole life was dominated by an all-pervading lust for power. Nothing mattered— truth, honour, or the keeping of faith—nothing, provided that he could gain and hold his personal power. Without doubt he had great gifts as an orator. He had an enormous belief in himself. He could, in spasmodic outbursts, work at intense pressure with a terrific outpouring of mental force. He had, of course, the advantage that a man devoid of any moral scruple will have over those whose conscience sets a limit to action. The early days of his movement were humble enough, and they were almost entirely conditioned by the circumstance in Munich. Between Bavaria and Prussia there had been dislike and suspicion for centuries. Now Prussia and the Weimar Republic had become almost synonymous. Ultra-conservative, Catholic, Bavaria hated to its core this Socialist hotch-potch of a Government which, in Bavarian eyes, had betrayed Germany, signed a scandalous Peace Treaty, and was doing nothing for the fighting soldiers.

In the meantime the Allies, and particularly France, were trying to get reparations out of Germany and were finding the task difficult. These difficulties arose in part, without doubt, as a result of German obstruction, but partly because the level of reparations had been set so high that fulfilment was economically impossible. In 1923 the French Government under the leadership of its Prime Minister, M. Raymond Poincaré, decided that German procrastination and refusal to deliver reparations justified the occupation by French troops of the industrial district of the Ruhr. The British Government did not agree with this action and did not send British troops to take part. The German Government decided to fight the French occupation of the Ruhr with the only means available— passive resistance and a series of strikes. This policy was, however exceedingly expensive, and it dealt the deathblow to the already seriously inflated German currency. Even before 1923 the German Mark had commenced a downward slide. Now inflation was becoming fantastic. So rapid was the collapse that prices changed overnight. Barrow-loads of well-nigh worthless paper were required to pay the wages in the smallest of factories, and the nominal quotation of the Mark reached a thousand milliard to the dollar before it ceased, in fact, to have any value at all.

It has been rightly said that inflation of this degree, the complete loss of value of a currency, strikes a blow which is more widespread throughout a nation than almost any other calamity. Families with a lifetime's record of careful and prudent conduct saw their wealth vanish overnight. The vast and class-proud German professional and middle classes were, in their own estimation, reduced to the standard of living of the industrial proletariat, a shock to the country's nervous system which was going to have a bad effect in the years to come.

It was in the middle of all this nervous disorder that Hitler and his group of discontented ex-soldiers seized the idea of capturing the Government of Bavaria. He had obtained the valuable, though eccentric, support of General Ludendorff and, through a certain Captain Roehm, Hitler had thought that he had been able to neutralize the army garrison at Munich. So, on November 9, 1923 a procession of National Socialists, with Hitler and Ludendorff, Göring and Hess, marching in the front ranks, moved through the streets of Munich towards the Government building. The Bavarian Government, however, had resolved that the time had come to put a stop to the bullying of this relatively small group, and a force of Bavarian State Police barred the way. A volley was fired; some of the National Socialists were shot and killed, including the man marching next to Hitler in the front rank of the column. Hitler either fell or was pulled to the ground by the falling casualties— the story is not clear. His shoulder was dislocated, and, in considerable pain, he was taken to the rear of the column and put into an ambulance. The Nazis broke up in disorder. It was a poor anticlimax. The only person who emerged from the fiasco with any credit was Ludendorff, who, correctly guessing that the Police would not fire on a general, strode forward, knocked up the Police carbines, and walked through their ranks. Hitler was arrested, was tried, was condemned to five years' confinement in a fortress. He was in Landsberg from November 11, 1923, to December 20, 1924. He was still an Austrian citizen, and he should have been expelled as an undesirable person across the frontier to Austria. Had it not been for the perpetual Bavarian dislike of the Central Government this would probably have taken place and world history would have been very different. As it was, thirteen months in Landsberg prison gave Hitler time to write *Mein Kampf.*

While Hitler was in prison the situation in Germany was improving rapidly. Dr. Stresemann, of the German Peoples Party (Deutsche Volkspartei), the German Foreign Minister, had decided to break off the costly struggle with France. The French themselves were glad enough to get rid of a very complicated situation. An able financier, Helferich, had planned a currency reform involving the cancelling of the worthless paper and the introduction of a new Renten Mark. After his death he was succeeded by one equally able, Dr. Hjalmar Schacht. The Dawes plan provided the first attempt to deal with Germany's reparation responsibilities on a sensible basis, the French troops withdrew from the Ruhr, and the Treaty of Locarno, signed by Mr. Austen Chamberlain for Great Britain, M. Aristide Briand for France, and Dr. Stresemann for Germany, seemed to usher in a new period of European co-operation.

The years 1924 to 1929, five years in all, were indeed a false dawn of a better day. Stresemann saw the only hope for his country in what was called the "policy of fulfilment."

In February 1925 the first President of Germany, the Socialist Ebert, died. In his place was elected the veteran Marshal Hindenburg, the victor of the battle of Tannenberg and the leader of the German armies in the West during the second half of the war. The fact that this upright, aged, Prussian soldier was prepared to be President of a nation guided by Stresemann and his policy was of enormous psychological help to the German Government.

During this period large sums of American money were flowing into Germany. In fact, in those days, money was describing a circle. Germany was paying reparations to the Allies, the Allies were paying their debts to the United States, and a substantial portion of this money was returning to Europe in the form of private loans to Germany or to Austria. Some of this American money was being reinvested through London or Amsterdam, but a great deal was lent by America directly to bankers, industrialists, or city authorities in Central Europe. It may be emphasized, at this point, that this large flow of money, in striking contra-distinction to Marshall Aid of a later age, was all private investment, not subject to Government check or control. Some of it was a long-term loan, much of it was money at short-term or at call. Without doubt, those who received the money in Germany or in Austria thought of it as being available for a long time. With this unexpected flow of gold, factories were re-equipped, large blocks of working-class houses were built, and trade was financed.

In the better atmosphere of this Stresemann period Hitler's propaganda could have only limited success. He did, however, secure during this time his most gifted lieutenant, Dr. Joseph Goebbels, a clever, able little man of good education, with a twisted foot and distorted mind. Goebbels carried the Nazi message into the back streets of the working-class districts of Berlin. It was a message of concentrated hate and dislike, anti-Semitic, anti-Socialist, anti-Communist, and anti-Stresemann. As always, Hitler knew how to tune his message so that it should appeal to those who carried a grievance.

In the elections which were held for the Reichstag in May 1928 the Social Democrats, the Party which had, in fact, been responsible for the Government of Germany for nearly ten years, secured 9.15 million votes. The Nationalist Socialist Party put up its own candidates. They secured less than one million votes—in fact, eight hundred and ten thousand—and got twelve seats out of four hundred and ninety-one that made up the full Reichstag. Their policy was, however, to receive some support from an outside source. Stresemann had continued his policy of fulfilment. The Kellogg Pact and the Young Plan, the entry of Germany into the League of Nations, had followed the line of policy which he had marked out at the Treaty of Locarno in 1925. But this policy had bitter opponents. A group of Rhineland industrialists, headed by Hugenberg, had thrown their weight and their money into the formation of a Nationalist Party, violently anti-Ally, violently anti-Socialist and, naturally, violently anti-Stresemann. Then on October 3, 1929, worn out by his efforts, Stresemann died.

Almost simultaneously across the Atlantic occurred an event that, in any case, was due to wreck all his hopes. In autumn of 1929 a crisis hit Wall Street. Over-enthusiasm and over-optimism had brought the American financial and industrial edifice to a very dangerous position. A severe recession took place, and American bankers, thoroughly alarmed, tried to bring back from overseas the gold which they had invested. By 1930 the crisis reached Germany. That summer unemployment reached three million. Hitler's propaganda could give to the unemployed a simple solution to their

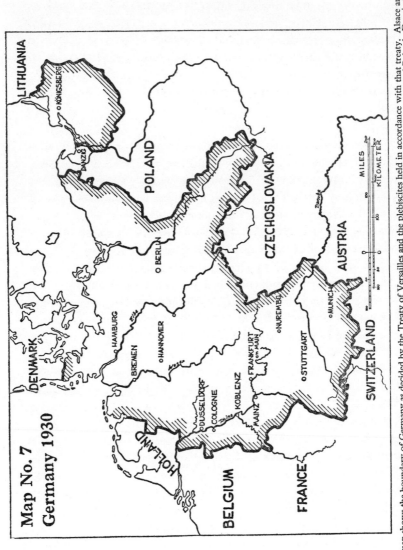

Map No. 7
Germany 1930

The map shows the boundary of Germany as decided by the Treaty of Versailles and the plebiscites held in accordance with that treaty. Alsace and Lorraine returned to France, Northern Schleswig went to Denmark. West Prussia, Posen and part of Upper Silesia went to a recreated Poland. Danzig became a Free City under League of Nations protection.

problems—it was to get rid of the Jews and get rid of the "system;" and by the system he meant the Government with its coalition of the Weimar Parties. In the elections which took place in September 1930 the Nazi Party scored six and a half million votes for their 107 seats.

To such foreign creditors as still had any faith in Germany this Nazi success was terrifying. The drain away of money from Germany continued. In May 1931 the foundations of Europe's credit were shaken when the great banking house, the Credit Anstalt of Vienna, closed its doors. This was followed, in July of the same year, by the failure of one of the Big Four of the German banks, the Darmstadter and National Bank, normally known by its initials as DANAT. Faced by this crisis the Government declared a moratorium. Brüning, now in charge at Berlin, tried in vain to get help from abroad, but other countries had their problems. It was in September 1931 that Great Britain went off the gold standard and Mr. Ramsay MacDonald was forced to form a National Government. It was at this time that the Japanese armies marched into Manchuria and challenged the post-war hope of the League of Nations.

The years 1931 and 1932 were for the Germans years of unemployment, misery, and intrigue. Those who see him at work today will be the first to admit that the German is a good and hard worker. But there is a reverse side to this picture; the German can put up with unemployment less patiently than perhaps any other inhabitant of Europe. By the end of 1931 there were five million out of work. Factory after factory was closing down for want of money. There was not only unemployment among the artisans and unskilled labourers. The whole of the vast middle class, the lawyers, doctors, banking officials, and the counting-house cashiers, even if still at work were fearful of what the morrow might bring, and were worried to distraction by debts which they could not pay. Moreover, unlike many other periods of unemployment, this time the crisis hit the countryside. Farmers were unable to meet obligations which they had incurred, perhaps light-heartedly, in the days when money was plentiful. Farms were being sold out all over the country, and farmers were being turned out of houses in which their forbears had lived for generations. In 1932 the unemployment figure in Germany rose to the colossal level of seven million, and of those still at work many did not know whether or not tomorrow's wages would arrive. In Berlin Brüning was trying to govern with the support of his own Party, the Centre, and the Democrats, with the usual, but not guaranteed, support of the Socialists. To provide the barest minimum of unemployment-pay heavy taxation was inevitable. It was equally inevitable that heavy taxation would be hated. In order to make his Finance Bill operative, Brüning, in the autumn of 1931, applied to the President for power to put a bill through by the machinery of an emergency decree. This was, in fact, to prove a fatal step, for it was to show the way to Von Papen and Hitler.

In 1932 President Hindenburg's term of office came to an end and he stood for re-election. With incredible political folly the right-wing parties put up their own candidate against Hindenburg. So great was their hatred of the Brüning Government that even the victor of Tannenberg was tainted in their eyes by the infection. Adolf Hitler announced that he would stand as candidate. To do this he had to obtain German citizenship, for he was still an Austrian. This was arranged for him in the small state of Brunswick where there was a local Nazi majority. Hindenburg received eighteen and a half million votes and Hitler eleven and a half million, but, by one of those evil chances that seemed destined to give Adolf Hitler an opening, the Hindenburg total was a few thousand short of the necessary two-thirds majority. A second election had to take place. Hindenburg was furious with Brüning who, in the President's eyes, was entirely responsible for the lack of loyalty of the right-wing parties. In the second election, Hindenburg received nineteen and a half million votes and Hitler received thirteen million. By now it was clear to Germany, to the world, and, above all, to Hitler himself, that he was a man of destiny in Germany. There followed a confused series of intrigues. Germany, as a whole, was in a state of national hysteria and very near civil war. Communist and Nazi processions were fighting each other daily in the streets. On May 30, 1932, Hindenburg dismissed Brüning and appointed Von Papen as Chancellor. On June 17 a street fight took place in Altona, then not, as now, part of Hamburg but a separate Prussian city. A procession of Nazis started from inside the Hamburg suburb of St. Pauli and provocatively marched down the hill into Altona's back streets by Kleine Freiheit, known to be a Communist quarter. The Altona Police authorities were caught unprepared, and there was a street fight in which nineteen were killed and two hundred and eighty-five were wounded. Von Papen seized this excuse to declare the Prussian Government incompetent and incapable, and he dismissed the Socialist Cabinet. This was the use of force against a parliamentary system. Years before, the German Trade Unions had defeated the challenge of the right-wing Kapp Putsch by the weapon of a general strike. Faced with this obvious threat of a right-wing dictatorship, the Socialist trade union leaders this time held their hand. With seven million unemployed, it was no time to risk the challenge of a strike. Once again the complicated German political machine was to call the electors to the poll. On July 31 elections for the Reichstag resulted in a Nazi gain. They had thirteen and three-quarter million votes and two hundred and thirty seats. Their vote was 37.3 per cent of the whole. By now the Nazis and the Communists together, the extremists of the Right and Left, were accounting for more than half the House. When Parliament met on August 30 the anti-Government parties, the Nazis and the Communists, joined on this occasion, and with great folly, by the Social Democrats, combined forces in a vote of censure and threw Von Papen out. Papen dissolved the House and appealed to the electorate. Again there had to be new elections. The Nazi Party suffered a set-back. Moreover the party was running short of money. Their vote sank to 33 per cent, and they held 196 places in the House: the Communists had 100. The German Parliament, based on a complicated system of proportional representation, was grinding to a standstill. Von Papen thought that the only solution was to rule by presidential decree, based on the Army's loyalty to Hindenburg. For a short time the aged President agreed; then, at a fatal discussion with General von Schleicher, Hindenburg learnt the unwelcome news that the Army, though loyal to him, did not feel strong enough to carry out the task of supporting an unpopular Government against Nazi and Communist attack. So, on January 30, 1933, after a further series of complicated intrigues, and on the advice of Von Papen, Hindenburg offered Adolf Hitler the post of Chancellor and accepted the Nazis as the strongest party in a Coalition Government.

It is sometimes thought abroad, and was often claimed by the National Socialists, that Hitler was swept into power by a great mass movement. He was not. He was, in the end, jobbed into power by a group of right-wing politicians of the old gang who despised the Socialists, feared the Communists, and thought that they could control Hitler. Some of them, including Von Papen, had the naive belief that, having placed Hitler in power they would be a match for him in a battle of wits and would be able to control both him and the new forces which he represented. The day of their disillusionment was near at hand. Göring was the Minister of the Interior in Prussia and the Minister of the Interior controlled the Police. On February 27th, 1933, the Reichstag building caught fire and was burned out. The origin of this fire is, even to this day, somewhat of a mystery, though many will believe the truth of General Halder's affidavit in the course of the Nuremberg trials to the effect that Göring told Halder in 1942 that he—Göring—had started the Reichstag fire. To the propaganda machinery of the Nazi party there was no mystery at all. They blared forth the categorical assertion that the building had been fired by the Communists. Based upon this false statement Hitler obtained from President Hindenburg a decree which bore the title "For the

Preservation of the State." This would give him power, when he required it, to take action to outlaw the Communists. In March 1933, under conditions of economic confusion, mental stress, tumult in the streets and the full blast of National Socialist propaganda, the German people elected a new Reichstag. Even so Hitler was only able to secure 43.9% of all votes cast. This gave him 288 seats in the Parliament. It is interesting to study the sources from which Hitler drew his support. He received over fifty per cent of all votes in East Prussia, in Silesia, in Schleswig Holstein, in the Regierungs Bezirk Stade and in parts of Thuringia. These were either frontier districts where national sentiments had been strongly stirred or from the areas of small farms where men were bitterly resentful of a Government which had, in their eyes, forced the agricultural countryside to be sold out in auction. Hitler received under thirty-five per cent of the votes in Berlin, Hamburg and the Ruhr. The German working man was still voting either Socialist or Communist. On March 23rd, 1933, Hitler presented to the Reichstag his Enabling Law. This, if passed, would enable him to rule Germany without a parliament. Out of the total number of 647 seats in the House the Nazi Party held 288. Hugenberg's Nationalists had 52. Together they gave Hitler a certainty of 340 votes. But a bill of such a nature as the Enabling Bill required to be carried by a majority of two-thirds of the total votes cast. This was the moment when Hitler brought into play the powers he had obtained from President Hindenburg "for the preservation of the state." He outlawed the eighty-one Communist members so that their votes were null and void. The Bill was supported by the Nazis, present in the house in their brown uniforms, by the Nationalists, by the Bavarian Party, by the Centre Party and also by the relics of the old bourgeois parties. The sitting of Parliament was held in the Kroll Opera House, it was packed with uniformed Nazis, and the S.S. men were in the surrounding streets. It was a matter of great personal bravery that men like Otto Wels, the leader of the Social Democrats, were prepared to go to the rostrum and tell Hitler to his face that they would vote against his bill. The Enabling Law was passed by 441 votes against the 94 votes of the Socialists.

That day, March 23, 1933, Adolf Hitler became the Dictator of Germany. The Nazi election campaign had been based upon bluster, intimidation and appeals to prejudice and hatred. Street fights against Communists and other political opponents had been the stock in trade of the Party's manner of life. Now that they were in power all the evil heritage of years of hatred and bigotry burst into the open. With no pretence of legal procedure tough squads of Nazi storm troopers beat up Socialists, Trade Unionists and anyone whose political views were obnoxious to the new masters of the state. In Prussia Göring had already established the State Secret Police (Gestapo) whose actions were declaredly outside the law. Within a few months of the entry of the Nazis to power concentration camps had been opened at Dachau and elsewhere. Some of the men sent to these camps were real criminals, but many more went there for no better reason than that their past record or present utterances did not suit the Nazi doctrine. In May 1933 the Trade Unions in Germany were dissolved and their funds confiscated. In July all political parties, except, of course, the National Socialist Party, were brought to an end. By the end of July laws had been passed removing from public office all persons of Jewish descent and all those who had shown any left-wing loyalties. So quickly did the Nazi leaders throw off the mask of legality. Setting aside the rules of justice, they proceeded to govern the country by their own bad standards. The concentration camps of 1933 opened a terrible page in history, which grew even grimmer and more horrible, till it culminated in the mass murders of Auschwitz. Between the night of June 29 and Sunday, July 1, Hitler by pure murder brushed out of his way Roehm, General Schleicher, and other political opponents who might have challenged his leadership. This was cynically known as the "Night of the Long Knives." On August 2, 1934, Hindenburg died. This time there was to be no election. Hitler announced his intention of combining in his own person the office of President and Chancellor. As soon as he assumed power he abolished the black, red, and gold flag of the Weimar Republic and substituted the Nazi Party's red flag with the black swastika on a white circle. The black, red, and white of the Bismarck Empire was also flown.

One German institution still remained not entirely controlled by Hitler. It was the German Army. Whether by combined action the generals could have repulsed Hitler or not is a problem difficult to decide today. It must be remembered that until March 23, 1933, the day of the Enabling Law, Hitler's rule had, at least outwardly, been established by constitutional means. Many of the generals felt that Hitler's policy of rearmament coincided with their own interests. For the first few years of his regime, the two forces, the old army and the new National Socialists, walked side by side. But Hitler never allowed anyone to share power with him. In the winter of 1937 he felt himself strong enough to strike at the Army. General Fritsch, the respected head of the German Army, was attacked on a trumped-up charge. He was dismissed in February 1938, and with him went sixteen senior generals. Blomberg also went; he and Fritsch were replaced by Keitel and Brauschitsch, men who would do what the Führer wished.

It was essential for Hitler's policy, as it was the inevitable result of his lust for power, that, having secured his grip on Germany, he should turn to the outer world. When he wrote *Mein Kampf* he explained to those who cared to read what were his ambitious designs for Germany.

Such of the history of the next years, 1933-9, as is concerned with the internal politics of Western Powers is outside the scope of this work. Nevertheless, one or two general aspects of the story may be emphasized. The first is that the period of time from Hitler's rise to power to the outbreak of war was very short indeed. It was in the summer of 1934 that Hitler, by a campaign of assassination, freed himself from all possible rivals. From then to his invasion of Poland was a period of just over five years. The second point to observe is that the early part of this period coincided with a time of difficulty for Great Britain. The world economic crisis had caused much financial strain and distress. It had also resulted in a reduction in national expenditure and serious gaps in the country's defence system. Public opinion on the subject of armament was very mixed. There was a good deal of pacifist and anti-militarist sentiment traceable to memories of war-time casualties. There was confused thinking as to the possible operation of the League of Nations. The League itself had already suffered a severe setback when it had been unable to check the Japanese invasion of Manchuria. In any case the absence of the United States from the Council of the League was an almost fatal weakness. There was a great deal of rather vague international goodwill in England, and men were reluctant to comprehend the full villainy of the Hitler regime. On the other hand there was a great wave of sympathy for the Jewish and other exiles who were being driven out of their German homes and were seeking refuge in Great Britain.

Therefore, for a number of reasons, Hitler's plans had a clear start of nearly three years before the seriousness of the threat began to be perceived in the United Kingdom. By that time Germany had achieved a lead in aircraft construction and Britain's diplomatic position was seriously weakened by delay in securing adequate air defence for London and other large cities.

Hitler confirmed his position as dictator in Germany in the summer of 1934. In January 1935 a plebiscite was held in the Saar region to decide whether this should or should not be German. The plebiscite was carried out in accordance with previous international agreements and in a strictly legal fashion. There was, however, a good deal of nationalistic emotion in the campaign for votes, and the very fact that the result showed a great majority in favour of Germany was an encouragement to Hitler in his policy. Later in that year the British Government decided that it would be wise to sign a Naval Agreement with Germany. The wisdom of this was doubted by many writers, including Winston Churchill. It was an important factor that France was not consulted and felt herself ignored by being left out of the discussions. Thus, at a serious stage of international affairs, there was a lack of understanding between London and Paris.

In 1935 Mussolini invaded Abyssinia. The British Government was faced with a really difficult situation. Public opinion was tending to demand a strong line of action in support of League Covenants. Yet the country's defences were not in a state to justify diplomatic risks. In 1936 Hitler marched his troops into the Rhineland in defiance of the Treaty of Versailles and announced his intention to incorporate the newly occupied provinces in his military defence scheme. Late in the same year the Civil War broke out in Spain. Italy and Germany supported General Franco; Russia supported the Communists. In September 1937 Hitler and Mussolini reaffirmed the Rome-Berlin axis. Now public opinion in Great Britain was really stirred. The Labour Party in the House of Commons, which had, up to this time consistently opposed the rearmament of Britain, now commenced to alter its policy. The Anti-Aircraft Defence of London was taken in hand with vigour.

Within Germany the speed and ruthless vigour with which Hitler had carried out his seizure of power had left his opponents divided and dazed. The Trade Unions were crippled by the confiscation of their funds. The Socialists were politically in a weak minority. The more soberly inclined elements of the moderate parties had no outstanding leaders. There were, from an early date, men of vision and integrity who could divine whither Hitler would lead the country but they were few and uncoordinated. Moreover as the Führer carried off with apparent genius one bold adventure after another the chances of successfully organizing public opinion against his rule faded away. "The sleepwalker with the lucky star" was, in fact, scoring successes for Germany, or so it appeared. Two men who early commenced to be the centre for small groups of political opposition to Hitler were Carl Friedrich Goerdeler and

Fabian von Schlabrendorff. Goerdeler came to the United Kingdom in 1937 and also visited the United States. The problem here was that though much informed public opinion was becoming thoroughly alarmed by the trends already evident in Nazi Germany, the serious weakness in the British Air Force and the deficiencies in the defence of London against air attack imposed an almost insurmountable restriction on direct action by Britain to restrain Hitler.

In the winter of 1937 a party of German generals made a study of Germany's military situation in the event of war. It advocated caution in military adventure. This formed the basis of a memorandum produced by General Beck in 1938. But Hitler could still silence these warning voices by the undoubted success of his bold strokes. In March 1938 he marched the German troops into Austria. They were welcomed by a large proportion of the population. Having thereby secured a position which threatened Czechoslovakia from three sides, he commenced a campaign of pressure on that country. Ostensibly he was defending the cause of the Sudeten Germans, settlers, mostly of Saxon origin, whose forefathers had come over the hills into the northwestern parts of Bohemia where they now formed a substantial proportion of the population. Acting in accordance with his sincere desire to preserve peace in the world and trusting that Hitler meant what he said when he stated categorically that this was Germany's last territorial aspiration in Europe, Mr. Neville Chamberlain agreed in Munich, in September 1938, to a solution of the problem which re-drew the frontiers of Czechoslovakia and transferred the Sudeten districts to Hitler's Germany. There seems to be fair evidence that some of the senior German generals were becoming gravely alarmed by the dangers of their leader's aggressive foreign policy. Whether they would, or could, have headed a successful revolt had Mr. Chamberlain been more firm in resisting Hitler's demands at Munich is a matter which has been much debated. As it was, the settlement was a victory for Hitler's policy and the opportunity for successful revolt, if it had ever existed, was shortlived.

Hitler lied to Mr. Chamberlain as he had lied to other people often before. In March 1939 he ordered his troops into what remained of Czechoslovakia. It was now clear that the situation was exceedingly serious. The full strength of the Goebbels propaganda machinery commenced to be directed against Poland, using the technique that had already been abundantly clear against the Czechs. Mr. Chamberlain attempted to steady the course of European politics, but the Pact of Non-Aggression signed on August 24, 1939, between the German Foreign Minister Herr von Ribbentrop and the Russian Foreign Minister, M. Molotov, made it quite clear that Mr. Chamberlain could expect no Russian co-operation for his efforts.

On September 1, 1939, the members of the German Reichstag were suddenly summoned by Hitler to a special meeting. In many cases they were fetched by special aeroplane or special motor car. When they assembled at ten o'clock in the morning they were told by Hitler that already, at dawn, the German armies and aircraft had invaded Poland. On September 3 Great Britain and France declared war on Germany. In a broadcast in German to the German people, on the evening of September 4, Mr. Chamberlain said: "In this war we are not fighting against you, the German people, for whom we have no bitter feeling, but against a tyrannous and forsworn regime which has betrayed not only its own people but the whole of Western civilization and all that you and we hold dear. May God defend the right."

The Polish campaign was not a long one. The Polish army, though it fought exceedingly well, was outmatched by the German tanks and mechanical formations. An unexpected feature, however, developed on September 17. That day Russian troops entered Poland from the east. By the time fighting stopped it was Russian troops and not German which occupied the larger half of Poland. Hitler was to find that he had to pay a dear price for Russian neutrality. In August 1940 the Baltic provinces, so long regarded as within the German sphere of influence, were incorporated in the U.S.S.R.

During the winter of 1939–40 the unreal war of the western front continued. Hitler was using the period to move his armies back from Poland and poise them for the next battle. Denmark and Norway were attacked on April 9, 1940. Luxembourg, Holland and Belgium were invaded on May 10. Italy joined the war against France on June 10. On June 22 the French Government signed the terms of an armistice with Adolf Hitler. But Free France, under the leadership of General de Gaulle, fought on overseas and underground.

Like other tyrants before him Hitler was now to realize that his own demonic fate could never let him stop. He had to go on trying to conquer the world until, in the end, the free world conquered him. Outside the range of his troops and his police all the human instincts of decency, liberty, and freedom were massing themselves against him.

The Battle of Britain, fought in August and September 1940, made it clear that an invasion of Great Britain was impossible. Throughout this period large and intact Russian forces were a menace on Hitler's eastern front. The strain on his nerves was too great and on June 22, 1941, exactly a year after the armistice with France, Hitler attacked Russia. He told his close ally Mussolini of his action when it was too late for Mussolini to make either protest or counter-suggestion. Now Germany was faced with that war on two fronts against which Adolf Hitler had warned the country in his political confession *Mein Kampf*.

On December 7 of the same year the Japanese, without a declaration of war, attacked the United States fleet at Pearl Harbour. That day Japan entered the war alongside Germany and Italy; the United States alongside the British Commonwealth, Free France, and Russia, and those other Allies, Norway, Holland, Belgium, Greece, who had never ceased to resist German aggression. As Winston Churchill wrote, "Many disasters, immeasurable cost and tribulation lay ahead, but there was no more doubt about the end!"

CHAPTER SEVEN

DEFEAT AND RECONSTRUCTION
(1942–53)

On August 31, 1942, Field Marshal Rommel, one hundred and twenty miles away from Cairo and at the end of a long line of communications, made his final attempt to reach the Nile. For five days his German and Italian divisions attacked General Montgomery's Eighth Army—a truly Commonwealth force, for it included South African, Australian, New Zealand, and Indian as well as British troops. At last, south of the Alam-el-Halfa ridge, the German attack died away. For Rommel, as for Hitler and Mussolini, that was the high tide of the success in the desert. Seven weeks later, on October 23, the British Eighth Army took the offensive in the battle known to history as El Alamein.

In the second of two great wars waged between Great Britain and her allies on the one side and Germany and her allies on the other, those seven weeks in the autumn of 1942 were the turning point in the military struggle. Winston Churchill has written: "Before Alamein we never had a victory. After Alamein we never had a defeat."

On November 8, while the Eighth Army was pressing Rommel's divisions westward over the old battlefields of the Libyan desert, powerful American and British forces landed at Casablanca, Oran, and Algiers. Operation "Torch" had been launched. Within a short time the whole of French Morocco and Algeria was secured for the Western Allies. Allied troops pressed westward and were

119

within a few miles of Tunis when the arrival of German reinforcements, coupled with winter rain and mud, slowed down operations. Also, on the other side of Europe's great battlefront, in Russia, the initiative was passing away from Hitler. In the north the German troops were still within sight of the suburbs of Leningrad. In the centre the front was now stationary, sixty miles away from Moscow. For a brief period in November 1941 German advanced troops had got within twenty-one miles of the city, but Russian counter-attacks and the winter cold had forced a withdrawal. To the south-east German armies had reached the Volga by Stalingrad and were on the slopes of Elburz in the Caucasus. The extension of the front was dangerous. German military strength was being overstrained by the demands of Hitler's strategy. The German general von Manstein has put it on record that he realized towards the end of 1942 that a military victory in Russia was no longer possible. General Paulus' Sixth Army, tied to the city of Stalingrad by Hitler's precise orders, had been completely surrounded by Russian armies on November 19. In mid-December Field Marshal von Manstein, with all the reserves of armour and petrol available, attempted, with the Fourth Panzer Army attacking from the south, to break through to link up with Paulus. The attempt failed and the German defenders of Stalingrad were doomed.

It was against this background in January 1943 that Mr. Winston Churchill, Prime Minister of Great Britain, and President Roosevelt, of the United States, met at Casablanca on the Atlantic coast of Morocco. There was now good cause for optimism on the part of the Western Allies. The long days of defensive fighting were drawing to an end and plans could now be made for the vast counter-offensive of the West. The opening moves of Montgomery's victorious advance from El Alamein and the Allied landings in North Africa had shown the way. Yet it was also clear that the direct Allied landing on the shores of France, the Second Front, so ardently desired by the Russian leaders, could not take place in 1943. The Allies did, indeed, plan to attack Italy in 1943, but a move from Great Britain across the Channel would require more massive preparation. In the meantime the Russian Government and the Russian people must be called upon to sustain the larger share of the military struggle.

It was not easy to explain to Marshal Stalin and his advisers why the Western Allies could not open the Second Front in France in 1943. There were, indeed, those at the Russian Headquarters who were inclined to cast doubts upon the genuineness of the Western efforts, and there were always Russian suspicions that the Western Powers might make a separate bargain with Hitler.

It was, therefore, necessary to give to the Russian Allies the most categorical assurance possible that Great Britain and the United States were prepared to fight to the very end to defeat Hitler's Germany. That was the mental background to the doctrine of "unconditional surrender" announced at the Casablanca Conference. It is important to note that this declaration applied not only to Germany but also to Italy and Japan.

It is argued by some German historians that the Allied declaration of unconditional surrender put a very powerful weapon of propaganda into the hands of Dr. Joseph Goebbels. They say that this doctrine made it exceedingly difficult for Germans to rally opposition to Hitler and his senseless conduct of the War. Winston Churchill's memoirs, on the other hand, make it plain that if the Allies had at that time, in January 1943, put down on paper their conditions for a treaty of peace with Germany these would have been very severe. In the existing state of public opinion in the United States and in Great Britain, such terms would have demanded the break up of Germany into separate states and the settlement of huge claims for reparations. Had these terms been committed to paper, the Allies might well have found themselves, at the end of a hard war, tied to a programme which was, in fact, quite impossible of fulfilment. In the event, when the time of Germany's collapse came, unconditional surrender was a formula of such simplicity that it compelled the Western Allies themselves to carry out the first steps in the reconstruction of Germany.

So far the three Allied leaders had not met together. In 1942 Mr. Churchill had visited Moscow. On many occasions he had visited President Roosevelt. Now suggestions were made for a meeting on the highest level. First, however, the three Foreign Ministers, Mr. Eden, Mr. Cordell Hull and Mr. Molotov, met in Moscow in October 1943. One of the decisions taken at this Conference was that a standing committee of Foreign Office experts from the three countries, the European Advisory Committee, should be set up in London to commence the study of the many problems which would have to be settled in Europe when Hitler's Germany was at last defeated.

This Committee met at Lancaster House, in London. Among the matters which it discussed was the problem of the military occupation of Germany. It had already been decided that this time, when victory came, the whole of Germany would be occupied by the Allied armies. This time there would be no partial occupation with a German Government operating in an unoccupied remainder. It would clearly be wise to decide well in advance which areas of Germany should be occupied by which armies. When two great forces were due to enter the country from opposite directions it was obviously prudent to decide where they should settle down. So the European Advisory Committee proceeded to draw lines on the map of Germany to delimitate the British, American, and Russian Zones. At that time it was not contemplated that there would be a French Zone. The members of the Committee were thinking of military billeting areas. It was the tragedy of later years that converted the boundary between army rest billets into an iron curtain.

Very shortly after the close of the Conference of Foreign Ministers in Moscow the three national leaders, Mr. Winston Churchill, President Roosevelt, and Marshal Stalin, met at Teheran. This was in November 1943. At this weighty Teheran Conference a great deal of the discussion concerned the active prosecution of the War. The Russians were anxious to know in detail the Western proposals for the opening of the Second Front for the invasion of France across the English Channel. But it was in Teheran that Mr. Churchill came face to face with a problem which, geographically far distant from Great Britain, was nevertheless to be of considerable importance to our history. This was the problem of the frontier between Poland and Russia. Already, on the occasion of a visit to London in May 1942, Mr. Molotov had raised the matter. Now it became evident that Marshal Stalin was going to attach a very great deal of weight to the Russian claim to reopen the issue. Three centuries of Eastern European history were moving to a climax at a conference held in the Persian capital.

In the wide expanse of country which lies between the city of Warsaw on the Vistula and the city of Kiev on the Dnieper there is no mountain range, no chain of lakes, nor desert which might make an obvious frontier between people. The Pripet marshes are a barrier to armies but they are not difficult to cross by tracks. There is a wide expanse of field, forest, and marsh with rivers wandering between deep-cut banks. Between the river basin of the Vistula, the heart of Poland, and the river basin of the Dnieper, the heart of the Ukraine, there lies a debatable land. It is marked out by the cities of Vilna, Minsk, Lvov (or Lemberg), Brest-Litovsk, and Bialystok. Within this area, sometimes in solid colonies, sometimes intermixed, lived Poles, Lithuanians, White Russians, Ukrainians, and Ruthenians. Most were Slavs, speaking one or other variant of the Slav tongue. The Poles were for the most part Catholic and used the Roman print. The Ukrainians and White Russians were of the Greek Orthodox Church and used the Russian or Cyrillic alphabet. In the early eighteenth century a great Polish kingdom had carried its rule eastward as far as the Dnieper. The Empress Catherine the Great of Russia drove westward the Polish frontier and brought White Russia and the Ukraine into the Tsarist Empire. How Poland was divided among Prussia, Russia, and the Austro-

Hungarian Empire at the end of the eighteenth century has already been told. For a brief period a 'Grand Duchy of Warsaw' under the protection of Napoleon revived the Polish nation. Then, after the Congress of Vienna, the Poles passed under foreign rule for a century. But even under the Russian Tsars there was a province of Poland. Both Napoleon's Grand Duchy and Congress Poland had centred upon the city of Warsaw and had been formed of the broad lands which drained into the river basin of the Vistula.

After the First World War the Allied Powers had decided to restore an independent Polish nation. To the west the boundary question was relatively simple. In general the boundary between Poland and Germany was to be as it had existed before the partitions of 1772 and 1793. The situation in the east was much more difficult to define. In an attempt to find a fair and lasting frontier between Poland and Russia, teams of Allied observers were sent to the area to question inhabitants and local authorities. Based upon their reports a line was set down on the map and recommended to the new Polish Government. This ethnic frontier has become famous under the name "The Curzon Line," called after the British Foreign Secretary at that time. It gave the town of Bialystok to Poland, the town of Brest Litovsk to Russian Ukraine, the ancient cultural centre of Lvov, or in German, Lemberg, to Poland. The "Curzon" line has imprinted itself on history. When Ribbentrop and Molotov reached their agreement in 1939 to divide Poland between Germany and Russia, the new boundary was to be not far from the "Curzon" line. So, today, the line drawn on the map of December 8, 1919, is very like the international frontier between Poland and the U.S.S.R. Bialystok is in Poland, Brest Litovsk in Russia, but so also is Lvov.

Perhaps sadly for history, the careful recommendations of the allied observers were not put to the test at the time. For war broke out between the new Poland and Bolshevik Russia. At one time Poles and Ukrainian separatists captured Kiev. Then a Russian army invaded Poland right up to the gates of Warsaw. At the moment of crisis, when the Russians were at the end of a long line of communication the Polish army launched a flank attack. The Russians were forced into a disastrous retreat. The Poles followed up, the Russians suggested peace negotiations. The two delegations met at Riga. Here the Poles succeeded in fixing a new frontier between their country and Russia. The "Curzon" line was dismissed as unfair to Poland and a new "Riga" line, about one hundred and fifty miles further to the east, brought the cities of Vilna, Pinsk, and Tarnopol and, incidentally, about six million White Russians and Ukrainians, inside Poland. The British Government of the day did not like the "Riga" line, and it was two years before it was recognized.

So matters lasted for nineteen years. Then on the eve of his attack on Poland Hitler reinsured himself by means of the Ribbentrop-Molotov pact with Russia. One of the terms of that pact envisaged a new partition of Poland.

Once war had been declared the advance of the German armies into Poland was rapid. It was, indeed, more rapid than the Russians had anticipated. So it was with some signs of improvisation that Russian armies moved forward on September 17 into Poland. The Russian Government declared that, the Polish Government having ceased to exist, Russian troops were sent to protect Russian populations. On the 18th Russian and German troops met at Brest-Litovsk; on the 29th the Russo-German treaty partitioning Poland was signed. The new frontier, this time between German Poland and Russian Poland, was not so very different from the Curzon line. The "Molotov" line did, however, give Bialystok to Russia.

Thus it happened that throughout 1940, while the battles of France and Norway and the air battle of Britain were taking place, German and Russian divisions were watching one another, each from one half of a dismembered Poland. That lasted for less than two years. Then, on June 22, 1941, great German armies moved forward, out of German Poland into Russian Poland, and farther into Russia itself.

In the winter of 1943, when Marshal Stalin met his two Western colleagues in Teheran, those German armies were deep in Russia. But the memories of the Curzon line and the Molotov line were very deeply graven on his mind. He wished an agreement from his two Western colleagues that when peace should come the boundary between Russia and Poland should not be the Riga line as it was between the Wars but should be the Curzon line, with Vilna, Brest-Litovsk, Pinsk and Lvov, the White Russians and the Ukrainians, all back in the Russian fold. But this was a very difficult question for the Allies, and, above all, for Mr. Churchill. For this involved a great alteration in the boundaries of that Polish state in defence of which Great Britain had gone to war with Hitler's Germany. There was an exile Polish Government in England. In Italy a Polish Army Corps under General Anders was fighting most gallantly in the army of General Eisenhower. Incidentally, many of the soldiers of this army came from those eastern parts of Poland which the Russians claimed for their own. Yet it was extremely difficult to refuse a request from our great Russian ally, whose armies were carrying so great a share of the armed fight against Hitler.

It was natural that the suggestion should be made that if Poland must surrender territory to Russia Poland should be compensated at the expense of Germany. Mr. Churchill has told how he illustrated his plan with three matches on a table-top. So already at Teheran the question of the westward move of the boundary between Poland and Germany was discussed. The line of the river Oder was spoken of as the possible Western boundary. Mr. Churchill suggested as a formula that "the home of the Polish state and people should lie between the so-called Curzon line and the line of the Oder." The exile Government in London were strongly against the surrender of land in Eastern Poland to Russia. They would have wished to have East Prussia but not necessarily any great extension of their land into Pomerania and Silesia.

Within Germany 1943 had been a year of disillusion and dismay.

It had been fundamental in Hitler's policy that the German people should have faith in his capacity to lead them forward to easy victory. He dared not speak to them of hardship, least of all of the possibility of defeat. Whereas, to the people of Great Britain on May 13, 1940, Mr. Winston Churchill was able to say "I have nothing to offer but blood, toil, tears, and sweat," confident that such a warning would evoke resolution and determination from his fellow countrymen, a year and a half later the German people were still being deluded by promises of early and glorious triumph. In the Sport Palast in Berlin on October 3, 1941, Hitler said, "I can tell you now—and I could not say this until now—that the enemy in the east has been struck down and will never arise again." A few days later, on October 9, Otto Dietrich, the Reich Press Chief, announced that the War in the east was over. These were vain boasts and soon disproved by hard facts. In the first week of November the German regiments, pushing forward northward of Moscow, had in fact reached positions only twenty-one miles from the city centre. Then, in a few days, the temperature fell far below freezing-point. Hitler had made no preparations for a winter campaign. The bitter Russian cold struck the German soldiery, who were completely unprotected, without warm clothing or shelter. For some weeks they hung on to their forward positions under conditions of great difficulty. Then they were pressed back by fresh Russian divisions coming from Siberia, well clad, well shod, and habituated to bitter cold. The hardships of that winter of 1941 are still vivid memories among German veterans. It is clear now from their records that, even in those days, the troops in the front line were beginning to have doubts in the wisdom of their Führer. Such doubts, however, and the state of affairs at the front came only slowly to the knowledge of the population at home in Germany. The few soldiers who came home on leave or were returned as wounded to tell their stories of hardship and lack of provision for a winter campaign were either disbelieved or their warnings were disregarded as being the isolated circumstances of one part of a huge battlefront. Throughout 1942 the propaganda of Dr. Goebbels' ministry was still able to maintain, among the bulk of the German population, faith in Hitler's leadership and in the eventual victory.

The great change came with the winter of 1942. In swift succession there followed news of Rommel's defeat at El Alamein, of the Allied landings in North Africa, and then, most terrible of all, the news of the surrender of General Paulus in Stalingrad with his army of 220,000 men. From then on there came to Germany nothing but worry and bad news. The Allies landed in Sicily. Italy concluded an armistice. In the last days of July 1943 British air raids on the city of Hamburg brought death and destruction on a scale never before witnessed. In a week of raiding, high explosive and incendiary bombs damaged nearly one half of all the houses in the city and killed 50,000 civilians. Desperate as the damage was, the rumours which spread all over Germany were even more alarming. The bombers had come and gone with very little interference either from the German artillery or from the German fighters. Later in the year there were heavy raids on Berlin. At sea also the battle was going against Germany. From March 1943 onward new Allied measures made the work of the German submarines ever more difficult. The figures of merchant ships sunk declined, the figures of submarines sunk rose heavily. By the end of 1943 it used to be calculated that of every flotilla of eight submarines that left German harbours only two would return safe and sound. In the end, the casualties on the German side were so heavy that of the 39,000 men who at one time or another served in German submarines 33,000 lost their lives.

By November 1943, therefore, by the time of the Teheran Conference, there were many people in Germany who had lost their faith in Hitler. Some, who had at first believed in the Nazi doctrines, had become thoroughly disgusted by the cruelty and the anti-Semitism of the regime. Others were beginning to see that the political leadership was creating a great legacy of hatred of Germany in the world outside. Some of the senior generals realized very thoroughly that Hitler's strategic conceptions were becoming more and more irrational and that his constant interference in military matters was disastrous. Goebbels reports in his diary that his post contained many letters asking why the Führer did not visit war-damaged cities.

Various groups in disconnected ways began to plot for a change. That Hitler should be removed from his position as dictator was already obvious to many. How it was to be done and what should happen thereafter were more difficult questions. Many among the best of those who opposed Hitler's evil rule would not contemplate assassination as a method. The officers had taken an oath of allegiance to the Führer, and, however much they now disliked and despised his leadership, they could not lightly break their bond. Several leading generals made angry protests against Hitler's leadership. The result was always the same: they were relieved of their commands and were replaced by men who would do Hitler's will. There was no concerted action by a group of senior generals.

There was a serious physical difficulty which confronted the conspirators. Since 1941 Hitler had lived almost the whole time at his battle headquarters called "Wolfschanze" (the Wolf's Lair), near the small town of Rastenburg, in East Prussia, some fifty miles south-east of Konigsberg. This was a heavily guarded military post. He seldom came westward into Germany, never visited a bombed city, and his public appearances became less and less frequent. Thus it became clear that the only people who could gain access to the Führer either for argument or for assassination were members of the armed forces or the National Socialist Party chiefs.

Now that all the facts are known it is clear that there were several attempts on Hitler's life. One of the earliest was on March 13, 1943, when a time bomb was placed on the aircraft which was bringing Hitler back from Smolensk to Rastenburg. The fuse was faulty and it failed to explode. One of the problems for those who were prepared to use the method of assassination was that it would be very difficult to choose a moment or a method which would remove Hitler, and, if possible, Goebbels, Bormann, and Himmler at the same time, without also involving the death of innocent persons—perhaps, indeed, persons favourable to the cause of the conspirators. As the months passed by in 1943 the number of those in touch with the plot increased, but so did the divergence of aims. Moreover, news of what was afoot had certainly reached some of those high up in the National Socialist movement. Several times during 1943 opportunities had been sought to kill Hitler but for various reasons could not be put into effect.

As 1944 opened, and the preparations for an Allied invasion across the Channel became clear, the urgency for action against Hitler increased. Field Marshal Rommel was now Commander of Army Group B in France. He saw clearly that Hitler must be removed if there were to be any chance of a negotiated peace for Germany. But he did not approve of assassination; he favoured the plan for the arrest of Hitler by the army, followed by an announcement of his abdication sent over the German Radio.

The Allies landed on the coast of Normandy on June 6, 1944. On June 17, at Soissons, Hitler arrived for an interview with Field Marshals Rundstedt and Rommel. The two soldiers tried to make Hitler see the seriousness of the situation. Rommel urged the Führer to seek a negotiated peace. Their efforts were in vain. Rundstedt was relieved of his command and was replaced by Von Kluge. Rommel thought over the matter further and wrote a letter to Hitler on July 15, repeating his arguments. Any chance that he might have taken action along his own lines was, as it happened, prevented by the Allies themselves, for on July 17 his car was attacked by low-flying aircraft, and he was wounded.

In the meantime those of the conspirators prepared to act through assassination had decided that time was urgent. They had got together a form of alternative government and they had made plans for simultaneous risings in Berlin and Paris. The man who would make the actual attempt on Hitler's life was Colonel von Stauffenberg, a seriously wounded war veteran. On July 20, 1944,

Hitler summoned a conference at Wolfschanze. Colonel von Stauffenberg attended as a member of the staff of Field Marshal von Keitel. He took with him a bomb with a time fuse concealed in his briefcase. He put the briefcase below the conference table, started the fuse, and, making an excuse, left the room. At 12.50 the bomb exploded. Von Stauffenberg heard the explosion, assumed that everybody in the conference room had been killed, and took an aeroplane for Berlin where he gave the prearranged signal for action in Berlin and Paris. But Hitler had survived. A stenographer had been killed outright and three officers died later of their wounds. Several more were injured. Hitler was badly shaken, his ear-drums were damaged, he was burned and bruised. But he was alive and in command of his senses. At Berlin Goebbels learned the truth by telephone from Wolfschanze, and at once took action against the plotters. By nightfall, in Berlin as in Paris, the conspiracy was at an end.

So the attempt had been made. It had failed, and it had failed in circumstances which brought the whole of the conspiracy to light. The consequences were terrible. The full force of Hitler's revenge, carried out by Himmler and his S.S.-men, swept away thousands who had only a slight connexion with the plot and many who had no connexion with it at all. It is estimated that some five thousand people were executed. Many more were arrested for varying periods. On October 19, S.S.-men called on Field Marshal Rommel. They gave him the alternative of a suicide which would be reported as heart failure or of arrest and trial before a People's Court. For the sake of his family he chose suicide. Hitler decreed that there should be a state funeral. Field Marshal von Rundstedt read the valedictory oration.

The revenge after July 20 had made any further plot impossible. It had removed the last chance of a peace by negotiation. It had made Hitler more insane than ever before and more than ever determined to pull Germany down in ruins around him when the last moment should come. The ten months that lay between the July plot and the end of the War were for Germany a nightmare of terror—terror of Himmler's secret police, of Allied air raids, and of the Russians in the east. Thereto was added the hysteria of Goebbels' propaganda of last-minute rescue through wonderful secret weapons or through fatal disagreements within the Allied camp.

Those same ten months, from the July plot to the end of the War, witnessed momentous Allied conferences. The picture was swiftly changing. The great adventure of the Allied invasion of Normandy across the English Channel had been launched on June 6, 1944. Two days earlier General Alexander's Allied army had entered Rome. Throughout the autumn of the year the German armies, fighting stubbornly, were being pressed steadily backwards through France and Italy. In Burma, as in the China Seas, the Japanese were giving ground before forces from the United States and the British Commonwealth. In this war against Japan, however, Russia was not yet a partner.

Therefore, because the main theme of the conference at Quebec was the prosecution of the War in the Far East, the talks which began on September 11, 1944, were between Great Britain and the United States. In the course of their meeting, however, President Roosevelt and Mr. Churchill did deal with two proposals affecting Germany. One was quite new in its content. It was a memorandum submitted by Mr. Morgenthau, Secretary to the United States Treasury, which proposed a radical reduction of Germany's industrial capacity, to the end that post-War Germany might never more be a menace to Europe. It went a long way towards converting Germany from an industrial to a pastoral community. The industry of the Ruhr was to be completely dismantled. The programme, if it had been carried out to its logical conclusion, would have meant the death by starvation of some five million Germans, for their means of life would have been withdrawn, and their removal by emigration in such large numbers would have been impossible. President Roosevelt and Mr. Churchill accepted the plan, temporarily, as a basis for discussion. It was, however, violently resisted by

Mr. Eden and other members of the British cabinet and by Mr. Cordell Hull and Mr. Henry Stimson in the United States. It never became part of the official policy of the Western Allies. Nevertheless it played a part in history. The contents of the Morgenthau plan became known in Germany. Dr. Goebbels' propaganda made most of the fact that the author of the memorandum was of Jewish descent, and the German people were told that what would be their fate if the Allies won the victory. In fact, however, the Morgenthau plan was not included in the official decisions of the conference.

It was different with another set of proposals. The two heads of government had before them the maps prepared by the European Advisory Committee, showing how Germany was to be divided into zones of occupation by the Allied armies. There was to be a large Russian Zone in the east, an American Zone in the south-west and a British Zone in the north-west. The Russian Zone, as shown on these maps, included those areas east of the river Oder and the Western Neisse which are now administered by Poland. At Quebec President Roosevelt suggested an alteration in plan, urging that the British and American Zones should be exchanged, on the grounds that the supplies for the United States troops and for the Zone could be more easily handled if they had the ports of the North Sea coastline. Mr. Churchill demurred to this change, and in the end a compromise solution was found, whereby the harbours of Bremen and Bremerhaven were allotted to the use of the American forces, and these ports, with a surrounding enclave of land, were regarded as a detached part of the American Zone. Paragraph No. 33 of the Quebec Agreement put the decision in the following terms: "that part of Germany not allocated to the Soviet Government for disarmament, policing, and the preservation of order" should be divided between Great Britain and the United States, according to boundary lines which were then set out in detail.

Thus the two Western delegates tacitly accepted the boundary line for the Russian Zone which had been worked out in London by the European Advisory Committee, a boundary line which has meant that today Magdeburg and the whole of Thuringia lie east of the Iron Curtain. Yet Paragraph 33 also made it clear that the Zones were intended as military areas for policing and disarmament and did not forecast the political dismemberment of the country.

President Roosevelt had to fight a presidential election in November 1944. So the next conference was also between two only of the three great leaders. This time it was in Moscow, where on October 9 Mr. Churchill and Mr. Eden met Marshal Stalin and Mr. Molotov. They discussed the projects for Russian entry into the war against Japan, they discussed the formation of a common policy for the Balkan states, and they also tackled once again the difficult problem of the Russian-Polish frontier. Representatives of the exile Polish Government in London had been invited to Moscow, and they met there the representatives of the other group which also claimed the right to represent Poland, the so-named "Lublin" Committee, men very much under Russian influence. There was little progress towards an amicable solution. The London Poles were very loath to agree to the Curzon line and especially to the surrender of the city of Lvov to Russia. The Lublin Poles, as was to be expected, supported the Russian view. All this was, before long, to be very important to post-War Germany. Yet, at Moscow, there was not much discussion about the shape of Germany in the future. The records show that even at this late stage, six months before the War ended, there was still discussion as to whether the solution should be a new state consisting of Austria, Bavaria, Baden, and Wurttemberg, with its capital at Vienna. In any case, it was realized at Moscow that a further Three Power conference must shortly take place. This was the Yalta conference of February 1945.

On November 7, 1944, President Roosevelt had been re-elected for a fourth term. He was already a tired and ill man. At Yalta, in the Crimea, the three great war leaders, Churchill, Stalin and Roosevelt, met—for the last time as fate was to decree.

Tremendous issues lay before them. The war against Germany was clearly moving to an end. The war against Japan was approaching its climax. Experiments in the United States with a new weapon, an atomic bomb, had demonstrated its great power, but it was still an unproved force. A landing on the main island of Japan might be necessary before the resistance of the Japanese people gave way. Such a landing, carried out by United States forces, might be very costly in lives. If Russia would enter the War in the Far East that would, in some measure, lift the strain from the United States. At Dumbarton Oaks, not far from Washington, a group of British, American, and Russian experts had been working out plans for a new world community for the preservation of peace, the United Nations Organization. If this new scheme were to have any chance of success Soviet Russia must be persuaded to come in, with good will, whole-heartedly, and as a welcome partner.

Seen in retrospect it is quite clear that the decisions taken at Yalta, important as they were for Germany, were dominated in great measure by President Roosevelt's desire to secure Russian participation in the War against Japan and his great enthusiasm for the safe launching of the United Nations Organization. It was against this vast background of world politics that the discussions about Germany took place. These covered four main points: the future form of a German state, the question of reparations, the eastern frontier with Poland, and the arrangement for the Zones of occupation. Only in the case of the last item was there real agreement.

The Western Allies secured Stalin's consent to the inclusion of France as an occupying Power. But the French Zone had to be taken out of the Zones allotted by the European Advisory Committee to the United States and Great Britain.

Concerning the eventual structure of Germany there was little discussion. In truth it seemed to the statesmen at Yalta to be so great and difficult a problem that they shelved it by referring it to the Foreign Secretary's Conference, with instructions to produce within one month a plan for the dismemberment of Germany. The prevailing feeling was that there would be a long period of joint

Allied occupation of Germany, and that during this time the eventual plan for the future shape of the country would be carefully worked out, for eventual ratification by a Peace Treaty.

The question of reparation payments raised great difficulties. Russia had suffered terrible losses through the German invasion. Marshal Stalin put forward a claim that the total of reparations to be obtained from Germany should be fixed at twenty milliards of dollars, and that half of this sum should go to the Soviet Union. The British Prime Minister had already seen the unreality of a reparations programme after the First World War, and he knew that the figures now put forward by the Russians were also unreal. But Stalin received some support from Roosevelt and the figure of twenty milliard was accepted as a basis for record, subject to Mr. Churchill's reservation.

Mr. Churchill records that, of the eight formal sessions of the Yalta Conference, seven were concerned with the question of the Polish frontier. It became clear that the Russians, with the support of the Lublin Poles, were going to get the Curzon line, with Lvov included, whether the London Poles liked it or not. In the course of their talks with the leader of the London delegation the Russians had suggested that the compensation offered to Poland in the west might take her frontier as far as the river known as the Western or Lausitzer Neisse. Mr. Churchill issued a strong warning against the unwisdom of such a course. The land which lay between the Oder and the Western Neisse was heavily populated by Germans. It was not a question of taking into a new Poland a stretch of land with a large percentage of Polish or Polish-speaking inhabitants. Either the new Poland would have to include a large, and probably not easily absorbed, German minority, or there would have to be forced emigration of several millions of people.

Churchill protested against the idea of such large-scale deportations. Stalin thought that the majority of the Germans would have already left before the arrival of the Russian armies. Mr. Roosevelt's view was that "Poland should receive compensation at the expense of Germany including that part of East Prussia south of the Konigsberg line and up to the line of the Oder, but there would appear to be little justification for extending it up to the Western Neisse." There was, indeed, no agreement between the Russian view on the one hand and the view of the Western Powers on the other. The lack of unity was masked by the concluding paragraph of the statement issued at the end of the Yalta Conference.

"The three heads of Government consider that the eastern frontier of Poland should follow the Curzon line, with digressions from it in some regions of five to eight kilometres in favour of Poland. They recognize that Poland must receive substantial accessions of territory in the north and west. They feel that the opinion of the new Polish Provisional Government of National Unity should be sought in due course on the extent of these accessions, and that the final delimitation of the western frontier of Poland should thereafter await the Peace Conference.

Now, twenty years after Yalta, there is still no Peace Conference. But the frontiers of Poland to the west have, in the meantime, taken shape as the result of single-handed action by Russia working through a satellite Poland.

Only two months after the close of the Yalta conference President Roosevelt died. He was succeeded by Mr. Harry Truman, who had all the benefit of the late President's expert staff but had not himself taken part in any of the big conferences. On April 25 United States and Russian armies met in the middle of Germany, at Torgau on the Elbe. On the same day the Russian armies surrounded Berlin. On April 30, with Russian troops a few hundred yards away from the concrete underground shelter in the Chancellery grounds, Adolf Hitler took his own life. The northern group of German armies surrendered to Field Marshal Montgomery at his headquarters near Luneberg on May 4; German delegates surrendered to General Eisenhower at Rheims on May 7; and the final ratification took place in Berlin in the early hours of May 9. The war in Europe was over.

But the problems to be solved were large.

When the fighting stopped Germany was in a state of physical and spiritual bankruptcy such as has seldom been seen in history. Hitler, in his madness, had decreed a "scorched earth" policy, the destruction of everything valuable in the path of the advancing Allied armies. Not all his orders had been carried out. The resistance of his minister Speer had saved some of the factories. In Hamburg the local commanders, at the risk of their heads, had refused to blow up what was left of the harbour installations or to break the great bridges across the Elbe. There were other such cases. But the chaos was very great. The governmental machine had almost stopped working. The officials, most of them members of the Nazi Party, were discredited. Many had run away, others were arrested by the Allies. Over much of Northern Germany railway lines and roads had been wrecked by the senseless last minute blowing up of bridges by the Volkssturm, the local militia. Trains were not running, banks were closed, the post office was not working. The Allied armies found themselves confronted with a situation where they had to take over the administration of the country down to the smallest details.

The British and American High Command had for two years or more been training Military Government staff for the administration of Germany. But the problem which now presented itself was far greater than had been envisaged. It had been fairly generally expected that when the defeat of Germany was seen to be inevitable, perhaps when Allied troops were firmly established on German soil, Hitler would then disappear. He would commit suicide, or he would be assassinated, and he would be succeeded by a German Government which would accept Allied orders. This—German—successor Government would, it was assumed, be located in Berlin. It would work under the very precise instructions of an Allied Control Council. Distributed over all Germany there would be

Allied Military Government officers whose duty it would be to see that the instructions given by the Allied Control Council to the central German administration were correctly carried out by subordinate German officials.

In fact things did not work out like that. The failure of the July plot, the revenge taken after its failure, and Hitler's mad determination to drag Germany down in the ruins of his own defeat meant that at the moment of that defeat it was not possible to set up a successor administration.

There were two other factors which did affect the situation. Just in the last weeks of the War the Allied armies, both British and American, had uncovered the frightful horrors of the concentration camps at Belsen, Dachau, and Buchenwald. These were later to be far out-horrored by the revelations of what had happened at Auschwitz in Poland. Nevertheless the results of these discoveries were to create, in the minds of the troops in Germany and the populations at home, a violent increase in anti-German feeling just at a moment when, in any case, emotions were tense at the end of a long and bitter war.

In his last broadcasts to the German people Goebbels had spoken of an organization to which he gave the name Wehrwolf. From his threats it appeared that it was to be some desperate plot for underground resistance to the Allies. In truth, in the light of present knowledge, it seems doubtful whether very much did exist outside Goebbels' wild words. But the idea that there might be in Germany a stubborn group of fanatics under the code name Wehrwolf was for a time accepted seriously by some Allied commanders and caused military precautions to be taken which were not, in fact, necessary.

For there was not the slightest sign of any German resistance movement. There was no sabotage, there were no acts of hostility towards Allied troops. Orders given by Military Government officials were obeyed, as efficiently as was to be expected in those difficult days. With the Wehrwolf threat in their mind this obedience was unexpected and perhaps distrusted by some Allied officials.

In fact, the German people were at the end of their nervous strength. Disillusionment, disaster, the terror of Himmler's execution squads after July 20, the incessant Allied air attacks, the hopelessness of the struggle, even the palpable falsehoods of Goebbels' newsreels—all combined to bring an entire nation to a state of mental exhaustion, where anything seemed better than the continuance of so much misery and despair. Moreover, there were many who genuinely felt that a better world could be built on the ruins of the old.

The armies of the Western Allies had halted on the line of the middle Elbe, though they could, indeed, have pressed on farther towards Berlin before they met the Russian armies moving westward. Still, the British and American troops were already well to the east of the line which had been drawn on the map by the European Advisory Committee as the boundary of the Russian Zone. Everywhere, in the Western Zones at all events, the armies were commencing to tackle the tremendous problem of first aid. Brigadiers organized countrysides; artillery sergeants, it may be, looked after refugee children. Large contingents of the surrendered German armies were moved back to their country fields to help with the harvest.

Three months after the German surrender the Potsdam Conference took place. This time the representatives of the three Powers were Mr. Churchill, Marshal Stalin, and Mr. Harry S. Truman. Mr. Clement Attlee accompanied Mr. Churchill to the opening of the Conference. Shortly thereafter a General Election took place in England and a Labour Government under Mr. Attlee came into power.

The situation that confronted the British statesmen was disturbing. At Teheran and at Yalta Mr. Churchill and Mr. Eden had resisted the Russian plan that Poland should take over German territory as far as the Oder and the Western Neisse. Yet they discovered that, behind the massive Russian armies, Polish officers and administrators were moving into Silesia, Pomerania and into part of Brandenburg—in fact, up to that Oder-Neisse line claimed by Molotov at Yalta. What President Roosevelt and Mr. Churchill had not agreed to in discussion was now in fact taking place. There was, indeed, little that the Western Powers could have done. Certainly public opinion at that time in England would not have approved of strong action against Russia to rescue German soil from Poland. Yet Mr. Churchill saw clearly the danger of this westward move of Russian influence.

More was to develop. It was decreed at Potsdam that the government of Germany by Germans had ceased. The government was to be vested in the hands of the four Commanders-in-Chief of the four Allied Armies—four because France was now associated in the plan. The phrase was: "Supreme authority in Germany is exercised on instructions from their respective Governments, by the Commander-in-Chief of the armed forces of the United States of America, the United Kingdom, the Union of Soviet Socialist Republics, and the French Republic, each in his own Zone of Occupation, and also jointly, in matters affecting Germany as a whole, in their capacity as members of the Control Council." Events were soon to prove that the instructions from his Government received by the Commander-in-Chief of the Russian Zone differed very considerably from those which were being applied in the Zones of the three Western Powers.

The basic plans governing Russian policy were becoming increasingly evident. The frontier between Russia and Poland had been moved to a slightly amended "Curzon" line. The frontier between Poland and Germany had been moved with Russian support, for it could never have happened otherwise, to the line of the Oder and the Western Neisse, with the city of Stettin, on the western side of the Oder, included in the Polish Zone. The next part of the programme was intended to make certain that the Russian Zone, with its western boundary deep across the middle Elbe and into Thuringia, should with speed and completeness be brought into the pattern of communist ideology.

However, at first it was possible to act with a certain measure of

Allied agreement. The terms for the quadripartite government of Berlin had already been drawn up by the European Advisory Committee and been signed by the Governments concerned. The city would be occupied by all four armies, British, United States, French and Russian, each administering its own sector of the city, with an Allied Commanditura to co-ordinate matters. Negotiations between the Allied Commandants in Berlin provided for the linking of Berlin with the Western Zones of Germany by corridors for air travel and by road and rail communications. The details of these arrangements were to be very important, when within three years of this meeting at Potsdam, tension developed between Russia and the other three Powers. The important decision of the Conference as to the administration and control of Germany have already been mentioned. Important regulations were also issued on Denazification, Demilitarization and Disarmament.

The British and American Allied Military Government in Italy had already soon learned that it was sheer common sense to protect themselves from "disease and unrest," as the phrase went, in the countries under their control. The same lesson was now learned in Germany. Therefore, throughout the first difficult years, Military Government, in addition to its work of Denazification, Demilitarization, and Disarmament, was also concerned with setting up a civil administration, opening hospitals and clinics, organizing railway services, and getting the post offices to start their work. In addition to this, medical stores and food had to be provided, even to the bare minimum required to protect Germany from a serious outbreak of disease. It is a matter of history that, due to the combined efforts of all parties to the programme, the Military Government health services, the Army hospitals, and the German civil organizations, there was no epidemic of disease on a large scale after the complete breakdown of May 1945.

The chaos due to war's destruction was serious enough. To that was added another problem, that of the Flüchtlinge—the refugees. There were three great waves of refugees which came into Western

Germany. First came those people of German stock who were evacuated from the Baltic provinces or from the extreme eastern parts of Prussia. These had left their homes in the autumn of 1944, under military direction. They had moved under reasonably well-organized transport conditions and had been able to take some, though not much, of their household goods with them. Later, in the spring of 1945, came that great flight of townsfolk and peasants who left their homes in Prussia, Pomerania, and Silesia before the threat of the oncoming Russian armies. In their case there had been no time for careful preparation. The family and its household treasures were loaded on a farm-cart and the sad trek westward began. Many died on the way, and many lost horse, wagon, and gear on the journey, but hundreds of thousands pressed on until they reached Schleswig-Holstein or the Luneburg Plain, only to halt when they came up against a thinner stream of refugees moving eastward before the British and American advance.

But not all the Germans left Prussia and Pomerania at this time. Many could not tear themselves from their homes. Many refused to believe the worst. Their time was to come a year or so later. Before the Second World War there had been prosperous German colonies scattered all over Eastern Europe. Till the poison of the Hitler creed was let loose on the world they had lived hard-working lives, at reasonable peace with their Polish or Russian surrounding world. Hitler's Herrenvolk doctrine had made use of them and German minorities had become centres of danger and areas of dislike. So, one of the decisions taken at the Potsdam Conference laid down that German minorities should be removed, back into Germany, from Hungary, Russia, Rumania, Czechoslovakia, and Poland. Hardly was the ink dry on this clause than it became clear that the Polish Government intended that it should apply to those lands which had only recently become Polish, the lands of Pomerania, Silesia, and Brandenburg up to the Oder-Neisse line.

From the Polish point of view this expulsion was essential, not only for the safety of the new Polish State, but also because their

143

Poland was surrendering great tracts of land in the east to Russia and would have to tackle the resettlement of millions of Poles displaced from east of the Curzon line. But the massed expulsion of peoples, envisaged by Mr. Winston Churchill at the time of Yalta, was going to be translated into the experience of real human beings.

In the winter of 1945 and the early spring of 1946 this German population was moved away from Breslau, from Glatz and Colberg and from many other country towns and villages which had been German in culture for centuries. These people were evacuated by train, taking with them just what they could carry and three hundred marks in money. The weather during much of this evacuation, known militarily as "Operation Swallow," was bitterly cold, and those who were thus evacuated suffered much hardship. The trains travelled slowly across North or Central Germany until they reached some small station in the British Zone, scheduled as their receiving station. There the fifteen hundred souls who made up the train load descended into a new, strange, and not too friendly world. Farther south, a somewhat similar operation was being carried out by the Czechoslovak Government, to rid themselves of those Sudeten Germans, the settlers in North-west Bohemia whose existence had given to Hitler his excuse for the campaign against Czechoslovakia. These Sudetens were mostly moved into Bavaria. Taking all the figures together, a total of some ten million refugees came into West Germany, raising the population from 38 million to well over 48 million within a matter of two years. It is worth remembering that this has constituted one of the greatest movements of refugee population which has been known.

In the summer of 1946, a year after the end of the War, Germany was still struggling out of chaos. The British and American armies were rapidly moving homeward. The United Nations Relief and Rehabilitation Administration, usually known by the initials UNRRA, was tackling an immense task in trying to find new homes for the hundreds and thousands of "displaced persons," those victims of the War years who had been carried off from their homes by German orders to work in German forced labour camps. In spite of heavy imports of bread grain, paid for by the taxpayers of the United States and Great Britain, the population of Germany was hungry. Food distribution was strictly controlled. The food value of a day's ration for the ordinary worker in the summer of 1946 was 1500 calories. Despite hard work by Military Government authorities and by German technicians and miners, the production of coal from the Ruhr pits lagged far behind what was necessary for the internal German consumption and for export to the rest of Europe.

In the meantime the Allied programme for Demilitarization and the destruction of German war potential was being put into operation. Because the British Zone contained the largest concentration of German industry, it was the British Military Government which had to carry through the largest part of the dismantling programme. As might be expected, this was unpopular among Germans and led to a good deal of local opposition and discontent. Nevertheless this most difficult operation was effected without any serious rioting and with no loss of life whatever. The German civic authorities and the German trade union officials exercised commendable restraint. The local British Military Government officials, and in particular, the Kreis Resident Officers had acquired by this time considerable local knowledge, and this, coupled with the regard in which they were held by the local population, made it possible to carry on with the programme until it was terminated by a change in the Allied policy.

It was during the summer of 1946 that the present federal structure of Germany commenced to take shape. Previous chapters have spoken of the traditional names of Prussia, Bavaria, Oldenburg, Saxony, Brunswick, and so on. The period of Nazi rule had, to a certain extent, reduced the importance of these old-established divisions, by spreading across the whole country the network of

Party groups, known by an old German word for the district, Gau. The leading Party functionary in each area was the Gauleiter. He was, in practice, the local ruler, and he took his orders direct from Berlin. Now, in the post-War Germany, the Allies wished to reduce the power of the centre and to give a federal form to the country. So they created new divisions. To describe them they took another old German name for an area—they used the word Land. The plural, in German, is Länder. So, in each of the Allied Zones a division was made into Länder. First, however, one decision of far-reaching consequence was taken, and this by the Allied Control Council itself. The state of Prussia was abolished. So vanished from the map of Europe the name Prussia, which, for good or ill, for two and a half centuries had meant something quite special and individual.

In the British Zone, after long and careful deliberations to which German advisers were called in council, five Länder were set up: North Rhine, with its capital at Dusseldorf, Westphalia, with its capital at Munster, Schleswig-Holstein, with its capital at Kiel, Lower Saxony, with its capital at Hanover, and the Free and Hanseatic City of Hamburg. This grouping meant the disappearance as units, of Oldenburg and Brunswick, both of considerable historical importance but adjudged too small for modern administrative purposes. The subdivision into five Länder was, however, short-lived. Within a few months it was held that the division of the Ruhr industrial area between the two states of North Rhine and Westphalia created administrative difficulties. So they were combined. The result of the union has been, without doubt, to create in Land Nordrhein-Westfalen, to give it its German name, a state which, with its twelve and a half million inhabitants, is rather too much a predominant partner in the German Federal state of today. It is interesting to note that these very important decisions were all taken on the responsibility of the Military Governments of the Zones, though indeed with much German advice. The British authorities took another decision which was a break with the past. The capital of the state of Nordrhein was fixed not at Cologne, the traditional capital city of the Rhine Valley, but at the newer city of Dusseldorf. The United States set up two great states of Bavaria and Hesse, with capitals at Munich and Wiesbaden. Bremen and the port of Bremerhaven were also attached to the American Zone. In the south-west, however, due to the somewhat artificial delimitation of a boundary line between French and United States troop areas, there were, for seven years or so, some rather small states. In the French Zone on the left, or west, bank of the Rhine, there was the Land of Rhine Palatinate, and that remains to this day. Then there were in the French Zone South Baden and South Württemberg, and in the American Zone the Land called Württemberg-Baden. Now, however, they have been joined, and there is a large Land Württemberg-Baden, with its capital city of Stuttgart.

It was a part of the programme of the Western Allies that democratic forms of government should be restored to Germany as soon as possible. Very soon after the capitulation town and county councils had been set up by Military Government. The members of these councils had been nominated by the Allies, usually after careful consideration of local advice. These men had done good work under difficult conditions and deserved well of their country. Now, however, the time had come in the autumn of 1946 for these nominated councils to be replaced by elected representatives of the people. The first elections were for the lower level of local government, for the Stadtkreise and Landkreise, or urban and rural councils as we should say. Included in this set of elections, however, by virtue of its special constitution, was the Free City of Hamburg.

It had been the aim of Russian political pressure to contrive a union between the Socialists and the Communists, to procure a "popular front," to use the technical term. In the Russian Zone they were successful. Otto Grotewohl, a Socialist leader of long standing, yielded to the temptation and joined with the Communists to form the Sozialistische Einheits Partei, the Party of Social

Unity. In Western Germany, however, the Socialists under the powerful leadership of their revered veteran, Dr. Kurt Schumacher, stoutly refused the Russian proposal. They saw clearly enough the danger that such a "United Party" might very well be used for Communist machinations in Western Germany and that indeed the entire popular front might fall under Communist control. Therefore, in these elections of 1946 in Western Germany, the Socialists campaigned on their own, and they forced the Communists to fight their own battle. The Socialists, the S.P.D., did well, especially in Northern Germany; the Communists, the K.P.D., had no great success anywhere.

It so happened that the winter of 1946-7 was one of the coldest and bitterest experienced in Germany for many years. The misery was great. Rations were small, rooms were unheated, electric light frequently failed, and public transport was sparse and over-crowded. Yet, in spite of all this hardship, there was little disease and no rioting. This winter in North Germany lasted late into April. By May 1947 the effective normal ration had dropped to 1000 calories. For the purpose of comparison it can be taken that the standard British Army ration has a value of 3400 calories. On the other hand the civilian population of Holland during the occupation of their country by the German armies were reduced to 600 calories a day. The economic situation was deteriorating rapidly accompanied with a mounting distrust of the paper currency. This was leading to unbridled traffic in the black market and a collapse into widespread barter transactions. To set against this grim background there were two developments of promise. In 1947 elections were held for the Assemblies in each Land of the British Zone, the Landtage. So, at this provincial level, democratically elected parliaments came into being and chose their own Minister Presidents. Also, thanks to the initiative of the American Secretary of State, the British and American Zones were fused into one economic entity. Later in the day the French Zone was added to form "Trizonia" as it was then unofficially called.

The year 1948 was to be one of destiny for Germany as for Western Europe. Combined Four Power action in occupied Germany had been increasingly difficult for months. Early in the year discussions took place in London between the three Western Allies and the Benelux countries. The problem to be studied was the association of Western Germany as a whole with the reconstruction of Western Europe and the establishment of some form of democratic government in Western Germany in advance of the time when the country could be considered as a whole. The launching by the United States of the European Recovery Programme, generally known as the Marshall Plan, with its hope for the impoverished countries of Europe, made forward moves essential.

In February 1948 the democratically elected Government of Czechoslovakia made the suggestion that their country should be a beneficiary of the Marshall Plan. The Russian reaction was swift and ruthless. The Benes government was overthrown by a Communist inspired revolt and a Police State was set up. To deal with that very real threat to Europe the union of states known as NATO was brought into being. The proposal made by the Western Powers that Germany as a whole should benefit from the Marshall Plan was met by a declaration by Marshal Sokolowski, the Russian representative on the Control Council, that any such proposals would constitute a breach of the Potsdam Agreement. Very soon thereafter the Marshal walked out of the Council Chamber and no Russian representative ever returned. That was in March 1948.

The breakdown of confidence in the paper Reichsmark currency had created a situation so desperate that most urgent steps were clearly necessary to avert a complete collapse of the German economy. American and British efforts to work out a combined policy with the Russian representatives came to nothing. The Western Allies therefore decided to carry through a currency reform on their own responsibility. The plan was not without risk and, in fact, the German authorities, such as they then were, did not feel strong enough to carry the burden of the operation. As a matter of history the currency reform of June 1948 was an outstanding success and gave an immediate stimulus to the West German economy. With the Deutsche Mark put in circulation against a sound backing in the West the Russians thereupon introduced their own currency into their Russian Zone. They also attempted to impose this currency upon the whole of Berlin, including the Western Sectors. This was seen as a serious threat to the position of the British, French and United States authority in Berlin and on June 24, 1948 they introduced their own currency into the city. The Russian answer to this was to impose a blockade on the avenues of approach to Berlin.

The two Allied Commanders, the American General Lucius N. Clay and the British General Sir Brian Robertson, on behalf of their respective Government, accepted that challenge and arranged to supply Berlin by air along the air corridors. Thus came into being that brilliant improvization known to history as the Berlin Air Lift. The goodness of Providence and massive American generosity contributed to help Western Germany. As a result of representations made by General Clay, large shipments of bread grains, amounting in all to three and a half million tons, paid for by the American tax payer, were shipped to feed the people of the Western Zones. That same summer Providence brought to the plains of North Germany the greatest potato harvest on record. Wheat and the other cereal crops were also good.

Thus it was that, in a few short months in the late spring and summer of 1948 the population of Western Germany received a new Deutsche Mark currency which they could trust, food to eat and strengthen their muscles and in the hundreds of great transport planes which passed over their heads a vivid reminder that the Western Powers had made up their minds to stand firm against Russian pressure.

It was in those months of the summer of 1948 that there commenced that national outburst of physical energy and mental determination which brought forth the economic rebirth of Western Germany. It is only fair to remember that it was a wonderful harvest, the American food-ships, the Allied currency reform and the Allied Air Lift which put inspiration into the deservedly praised hard work and enterprise on the part of the people.

Since Four Power Government had been brought to a standstill by the Russian withdrawal from the Control Council, the Western Powers decided that they must carry through their own programme for German self-government. A further conference between representatives of Britain, France and the United States, and the "Benelux" Powers, Belgium, the Netherlands and Luxembourg, took place in London on May 1948. On June 1, the last day of that conference, they confirmed their decision to proceed to the creation of a West German State. Following thereon the three western occupying powers established in September a German Parliamentary Council, consisting of sixty-five members nominated by the Länder Governments with five non-voting members representing West Berlin. It was the duty of this Council to work out a constitution for the new state. Discussions continued throughout the autumn of the year and then, in the spring of the year 1949 the full Council approved the Grundgesetz the Basic Law for the new Federal Republic of Western Germany.

On August 14, 1949, the people of Western Germany went to the polls to elect their own parliament. From these elections the Christian Democrats emerged as the strongest party. In coalition with the Free Democrats they formed the first post-War ministry. Professor Heuss, a Protestant and a Free Democrat, was elected President; Dr. Adenauer, a Catholic and the leader of the Christian Democrats, was elected Federal Chancellor. With a duly elected central German Government in Bonn, the time had come to convert Military Government into a Civil Control Commission. This was carried through by an edict of September 21, 1949.

It was in June 1950 that North Korean armies crossed the frontier and advanced on Seoul. This caused reactions in Germany as in other countries. Dr. Adenauer was concerned at the possibility of a

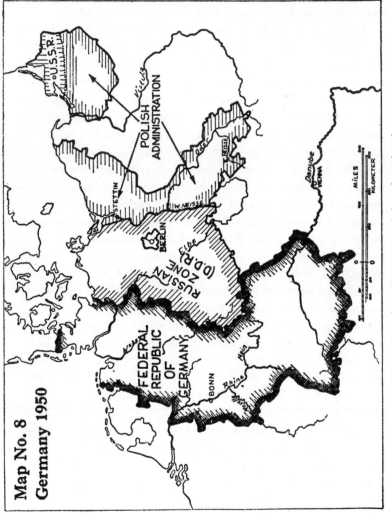

Map No. 8
Germany 1950

The map shows the administrative boundaries as they exist today.

152

similar invasion of West Germany by the large forces of Russian-trained police known to exist in Eastern Germany. He asked for power to raise a strong Federal gendarmerie. Although the Allies found themselves unable to agree to this, they were in a position to assure Dr. Adenauer that any invasion by East German Police would be met by action by the Allied troops stationed in Germany. Ever since the days of the airlift there had been a steady reinforcement of Allied troops, and the British army, which had sunk at one time to a strength of one formed Division, was soon to reach four Divisions, three of which were armoured.

The next development arising out of the Korean situation was destined to have a decisive effect on the Allied policy in Germany. Press messages from Washington reported that American experts considered that a contribution of twelve German Divisions was necessary in order to render effective the defence of Western Europe against advance by Russian land forces. Not unnaturally many German politicians were quick to see the bargaining power thus placed in their hands. Equally naturally, French politicians saw the danger of a recreated German army. Out of those difficulties the Pleven Plan, called after the French Minister of War, was created, the plan which afterwards expanded in the European Defence Community. For nearly two years discussions continued at Bonn. The Allies as well as the Germans had to work out a plan for the future of Western Germany which should include an effective defence of the West and take into account those fears which many felt in the face of the prospect of a rearmed Germany. Moreover there were in existence quadripartite agreements with Russia. It was in the interests of the Western Allies as well as of Western Germany that any new development should conform as far as possible with existing Four Power arrangements. The outcome of months of discussion took the form of the Bonn Conventions, treaties which would bring to an end the control of the Allied High Commission and would restore sovereignty to Germany, subject to a pledge on the part of Western Germany that she would enter the European Defence Community. This series of treaties received in May 1952 the signatures of Mr. Eden for Great Britain, M. Schuman for France, Mr. Dean Acheson for the United States, and Dr. Konrad Adenauer for Germany.

At the close of the summer of 1952 the Bonn Treaties had been ratified by the Senate of the United States and by the Parliament of Great Britain. Within Germany the completion of the Treaty was complicated by a question of constitutional law. On May 15, 1953, the Bundesrat approved the Treaty. Four days later the Bundestag, the Lower house of parliament ratified the Treaty by a good majority but not by a two thirds of the members of the house. It was claimed by the opposition that the treaties, and particularly those clauses which referred to military service, constituted a change in the Basic Law of the Federal Republic, the Grundgesetz. The question was referred to the Constitutional Court for advice but, in the meantime, events in the outer world were playing their part. In the first place it became clear that the treaties were not going to have a swift passage through the French Chamber. More dramatic were the events of June 17, 1953. That day there took place in the Eastern Sector of Berlin and in the Russian Occupied Zone a series of mass demonstrations which showed clearly a weight of public feeling against the authorities of the Eastern Zone. The news of these revolts brought forth strong reaction in Western Germany and there was a natural desire to make manifest national solidarity.

Meanwhile, under the leadership of Dr. Erhard, the Federal Minister for Economics, and Dr. Schaffer, the Minister for Finance, the commercial and monetary strength of Germany had shown steady and definite improvement. Export trade figures were excellent. The national currency, the Deutsche Mark was stable and commanded international respect. The unemployment figures were not alarming considered against the background of ten million "Flüchtlinge." The real value of wages was rising. On the whole there was peace in industry. There were few strikes. Directors and workpeople were co-operating in the rebuilding of their factories and shipyards and the regaining of their lost export markets.

With these considerations in mind Dr. Adenauer decided not to force the issue of the validity of the vote in favour of the passage of the Bonn Treaty. He saw the advantages of awaiting the outcome of the elections which were due to take place on Sunday, September 6, 1953, trusting that these would allow him to form a government which would command the necessary two thirds majority in Parliament. As the election drew near he appealed to the people of Western Germany for a vote of confidence in his policy both at home and abroad. In the field of foreign affairs he had stood for the closest co-operation with the West and for the effective integration of the countries of Western Europe. It was under his leadership that Germany had joined the Schuman Plan and had sent delegates to the Council of Europe at Strasbourg. The elections took place against a background of steadily improving standards of living. Thanks in part to Dr. Adenauer's personal prestige, the nation was acquiring an honourable status in the world. Even to the east the horizon seemed somewhat brighter. Josef Stalin had died in March of the year and the grim power of the Kremlin seemed not so menacing as before. In May Mr. Winston Churchill had spoken of the desirability of a meeting of world statesmen at the highest level, a "Summit" meeting.

The outcome of the election was a notable victory for Dr. Adenauer and his policy. Indeed it is worth putting on record that he received a far higher proportion of the popular vote than had ever been given to Adolf Hitler in the days when elections were still free. The Chancellor was able to form a coalition under his leadership which did command a two thirds majority. The two linked Treaties of Bonn and Paris were passed through the Bundestag on March 19, 1954, and through the Bundesrat on May 18 of the same year.

CHAPTER EIGHT

A SOVEREIGN STATE
(1954–64)

THE high hopes which had been built up in Western Germany in the closing months of the year 1953 were destined to receive a series of disappointments in the following year. Some indication of the difficulties ahead became manifest when the Foreign Ministers of the four occupying powers, Mr. Dulles for the United States, Mr. Molotov for Russia, M. Bidault for France and Mr. Anthony Eden for Great Britain, met together at the Berlin Conference of January and February 1954. It was soon made clear that while the three western delegates regarded the holding of free elections in the Russian controlled Eastern Zone of Germany as a prerequisite for any solution which dealt with Germany as a whole, the instructions given to Mr. Molotov were categorically against any such elections in the Russian zone. The Conference ended without any positive achievement.

It was as far back as May 1952 that the group of treaties known collectively as the Bonn Convention had been initialled by the statesmen of Great Britain, France, the United States and Federal Germany. Two years after that ceremony they had been ratified by three of the parties only, the confirmation of France was still lacking. As the months of 1954 passed by it was evident that the passage of the Convention through the French Parliament was going to occasion a bitter political struggle. Eventually, on August 30, 1954, the National Assembly, the Lower House of the French Parliament, by 319 votes to 254 refused to ratify the Bonn Conventions.

This refusal was a bitter disappointment for Dr. Adenauer whose whole policy had been based on co-operation with the West. It was a set-back to all those who had hoped to see European unity cemented by improved relations between France and Germany. At this crisis Anthony Eden, the British Secretary of State for Foreign Affairs, took the initiative. As a result of a rapid tour of the capital cities of Western Europe he found support for an alternative plan, a Western European Union, less closely organised than the first conception of the European Defence Community, but one into which Germany might be more easily introduced. As a result of his exertions a conference was held in London between September 28 and October 3, 1954. It was attended by Belgium, Canada, France, Federal Germany, Italy, Luxembourg, the Netherlands, the United States and the United Kingdom. To emphasize British determination to co-operate in the defence of Europe he announced, on September 28, his country's undertaking to maintain on the Continent of Europe, for the foreseeable future, four divisions of troops and a tactical air force, or other future formations of equivalent fighting value. This British declaration had the desired effect of reassuring both France and Germany. The United Kingdom, the United States and France then announced their intention to bring to an end the Occupation regime in Germany. Federal Germany would be a member of the Brussels Treaty Organization and, subject to the approval of all the other member states, she would join the North Atlantic Treaty Organization. She would re-arm within the framework of the NATO forces and would accept certain voluntary limitations on the type of arms and equipment to be possessed. There was also a complicated and hard-fought agreement with France concerning the future of the Saar territory.

These important decisions were worked out in detail by the experts of the participating countries and were then embodied in treaty form. It was in Paris, on October 20, 1954, that Eden, Dulles, Mendes-France and Adenauer approved the terms of the Treaty and it was confirmed by a Nine Power Conference the following day.

It was a condition of the Paris Treaties, as they came to be called, that they must be ratified by all the countries concerned before they could be operative. On this occasion Dr. Adenauer felt that he must await the decision of the French Chamber before he could put the question to his own people. Indeed the debate in Paris was long and bitter but in the last days of 1954 the agreement of the Chamber was secured.

The danger of another French refusal to ratify having been thus removed the Chancellor was able to submit four bills to the Bundestag at Bonn. The first ratified the agreement which brought to an end the Allied Occupation of Germany. The second dealt with the stationing of foreign troops on German soil. The third provided for the entry of the Federal Republic into the Western European Union and into the North Atlantic Treaty Organization. The fourth bill, the most hotly debated, covered the agreement reached with France over the Saar. The four were then further debated in the Bundesrat, the Upper House of the German Constitution, where the representatives of the Länder Governments had their say. There agreement was achieved on March 18. President Heuss signed the bills on March 24 and, on the appointed day, May 5, 1955, the Federal Republic of Western Germany regained the status of a sovereign state. Four days later Dr. Adenauer took his seat as a member of the North Atlantic Council in Paris. Thus, ten years after the defeat of Hitler's Germany, the Federal Republic, by the free vote of the democratically elected parliaments of many nations, was admitted into equal partnership with her former enemies. The Allied High Commission ceased to exist. The former High Commissioners became Ambassadors, Land Commissioners were Consuls General. The American, Belgian, Canadian, and other NATO troops stationed on German soil were henceforward there by virtue of a treaty with Germany and not as forces of occupation.

The reaction from Russia was that which might be expected. Their own creation, the communist government of the Eastern Zone was given a show of independence as the German Democratic Republic.

Federal Germany, under the leadership of Dr. Adenauer, was now free to conduct her own policy towards the outer world. It was a policy which was based upon a steadily improving internal position with a secure majority in parliament, a firm currency and expanding export trade. Towards the west Dr. Adenauer wished to continue a programme of close association with European movements and he laid a special emphasis on the spirit of reconciliation with France, a subject dear to his own heart. Towards the east his policy was one of caution. The closely linked problems of the Reunification of Germany, the status of Berlin and the existence of the Oder-Neisse line as the frontier between Germany and Poland were all highly charged with national and international importance. It was to prove impossible to disentangle them from the atmosphere of the Cold War.

In his thoughts towards a united Europe the Chancellor was reflecting the emotions of German youth. The movement for "Europa Union" had undoubtedly seized the imagination of the newer generation. So when at Messina in June the urgings of M. Spaak and the support of the Benelux countries launched upon a somewhat tepid Europe the concept of a Common Market this was welcomed by a fair proportion of the people of Germany. There was also welcome for the news of the conclusion of the Peace Treaty with Austria an agreement which seemed to show signs of a more liberal policy on the part of Soviet Russia.

This picture was darkened in a few months. Between July 18th and the 23rd the long awaited "Summit" meeting took place at Geneva. It was attended by President Eisenhower for the United States, Sir Anthony Eden, who had become Prime Minister of Great Britain, M. Faure the Premier of France and Marshal Bulganin and Mr. Khruschev the representatives of Russia. At the onset a dispute arose on the question of the inclusion of the re-unification of Germany as an item in the agenda. The Russians refused to allow this and the whole conference broke up without any real progress having been made. The Soviet contention was that the whole question of German reunification was a matter of no immediate urgency. Moreover it was evident that they wished to make clear to the East German Government of Herr Ulbricht and to the whole world that Russia was not going to make a deal with the west at the expense of the East Germans. On their return journey from Geneva to Russia the two delegates passed through Eastern Germany and there Marshal Bulganin made a speech wherein he emphasized for the benefit of his hearers the great weight that the Kremlin attached to the continuance of the Communist institutions and way of life as it had developed in the former Eastern Zone.

One matter which had greatly exercised German public opinion was the existence in Russia of numbers of German prisoners of war kept there as labourers even ten years after the termination of hostilities. The numbers mentioned in conversations were very large though many realized in their hearts that the bulk of those carried in the thoughts of friends or relatives had probably died years before. In the last months of the war, perhaps in the last half year, the administrative system of the German army had been swamped by the details of casualties and many of those regarded as missing were in fact killed in action or had died of wounds. Many thousands of others, alive at the end of fighting, but wounded or perhaps sick, had died in the course of the long transport into Russian captivity. Others had died in the intervening ten years. Nevertheless Germans hoped for the return out of Russia and Siberia of many tens of thousands of their fellow countrymen. This was one of the reasons which caused Dr. Adenauer and his colleagues to undertake a journey to Moscow in August and September 1955.

He was able to secure the return of the German P.O.W.s, but the numbers were painfully few. He was also able to arrange for the resumption of diplomatic relations between the two countries. Perhaps, however, the strongest impression made on the delegation was the contrast between the cordial relations which governed dealings between Germany and the Western Powers and the cool, indeed hostile, attitude which they encountered in Moscow. Perhaps the delegation from Bonn should have expected this, in fact it came as a shock.

For the next two years the relations between Bonn and the Kremlin reflected the ebb and flow of sentiment in the larger scene of the Cold War between East and West. Towards the end of 1955 there was a second Geneva conference of Foreign Ministers but it did not succeed in resolving the German problems. In the early autumn of the following year public opinion was buoyed up by the early news of political changes in Poland. It seemed as though Russia was prepared to accept a more liberal regime. Then came the terrible news of a popular revolt in Hungary and its ruthless suppression by Russian troops. Great sympathy for the people of Budapest was mingled with a realization of helplessness in face of a tragedy. There was very great bitterness in the Federal Republic.

The balance sheet of the year 1957 showed both credit and debit entries. The signature of the Treaty of Paris marked a great move forward in the concept of European unity. The Polish Government produced the "Rapacki" Plan for reducing tension in Central Europe which did contain interesting ideas. Then, with October 1, came the news of the successful launching of the first Sputnik. Russia had, it appeared, secured a technical victory over the United States and this was reflected in a tougher diplomatic attitude. There was tension in the Middle East which reacted on relations between the West and the East. Within Federal Germany elections again took place and for the third time Dr. Adenauer was elected Federal Chancellor.

The year 1948 had been a time of destiny for post-War Europe. It appeared that 1958 might prove to be equally dramatic. Perhaps reflecting Russia's successes in the technique of space travel the policy of the Kremlin was directed with increasing menace against the position of the Western Powers in the city of Berlin. A threatening speech by Khruschev on November 10 was followed by a note, eight thousand words long, delivered on November 27 to the Ambassadors of Britain, the United States, France and Federal Germany. The terms were strong, West Berlin was described as a "cancerous growth." Berlin was to be a free city. At the end of six months the government of East Germany, the German Democratic Republic, would exercise full sovereignty over the approaches to Berlin. May 27, 1959 was to be the day of decision "Everybody out of Berlin or else we shall push you out." Ten days after the delivery of this threat elections were held in Berlin. The "Unity" party which purported to represent Communists and Socialists working in harmony, secured only 1.9 per cent of the popular vote. The German Socialist party which had governed the city for years had an absolute majority of 52.6 per cent of votes cast.

Early in the following year, on January 9, the President of the United States in his traditional address to the two Houses on the "State of the Union," left no doubt in the minds of his hearers as to the force of American reaction to the Russian threat: "Not only the integrity of a single city but the hope of "all free people is at stake." Before the month was out there were signs of caution in the Kremlin. On January 24 Mr. Mikoyan denied that there had been any ultimatum intended in the note of November 27. At the end of February and the beginning of March Mr. Harold Macmillan who had succeeded Anthony Eden as Prime Minister of Great Britain went to Russia. He was assured that there was no intention to precipitate an urgent crisis. Khruschev was invited to visit the United States and he made a tour under conditions of considerable publicity. The "atmosphere of Camp David" was regarded as helpful. But a meeting arranged between the two heads of state, Eisenhower and Khruschev at Geneva was not a success. The "U.2" incident intervened. An American high-altitude aeroplane was brought down while flying deep into Russian territory. This event excited public opinion on both sides of the Cold War and caused considerable coldness between the two heads of State.

Sometimes it appeared to anxious observers that the peace of the world hung on a tenuous thread. Yet the year 1959 went by without any dramatic Russian assault upon the Allied position in the city of Berlin. 1960 brought with it a change in the Presidency of the United States. Mr. John Kennedy replaced General Eisenhower. It was thought by many that an opportunity might thereby arise for a new attempt to settle, by personal discussion, the many points of divergent view between East and West. Moreover the Lenin Birthday celebrations in Moscow had revealed to an interested world the depth of the political differences between Moscow and Peking.

Yet when the two heads of state, Kennedy and Khruschev, did meet in Vienna in June 1961 it was differences rather than points of agreement which dominated the conference. The Russians made it clear that they had four conditions which were to them essential for any agreement upon Germany: The Recognition of the Oder-Neisse line as the boundary between Poland and Germany, The Recognition of the German Democratic Republic, the D.D.R., as an independent state, the Clarification of the Status of Berlin and the Renunciation by the West of Nuclear Rearmament. The conference from which some advance had been expected broke up in an atmosphere of disappointment and disillusion.

The failure of the June conference added to the despair of many inhabitants of Eastern Germany. Over many years there had been a stream of refugees crossing from east to west. After the land frontiers had been closed and the passage into Lower Saxony or Hesse had become increasingly perilous, the only means of escape was through the middle of the city of Berlin. The passage from the Russian controlled eastern sector and the Allied controlled western sectors was subject to check but it was possible and those who sought in this way political asylum could be taken by air from the city to the

Federal Republic. In the summer of 1961 the numbers of those crossing from the east to west sectors in Berlin rose and the figures received considerable publicity in the world press. In the first six months of 1961 over one hundred thousand people crossed in this way, in the month of July alone the figure exceeded thirty thousand. This open evidence of discontent among the people of Eastern Germany and lack of faith in a communist regime was clearly very distasteful to the government led by Herr Ulbricht and to the Russians.

The month of August saw a continuance of the flow, by the twelfth of the month fifteen thousand had crossed. Then, on August 13, 1961 the East German Government sealed off their side of Berlin from the remainder of the city by the erection of a continuous barrier. Within a short time the first temporary obstacle was replaced by a solid wall. The whole operation was reported by television cameras to the homes in Western Germany and by film to the outside world. There were some who thought that there should be immediate physical counter action by the Adenauer Government or by the Western Powers. What might then have happened is a question still debated. In fact, however, no further action on either side followed the building of the tragic Berlin Wall.

Since then there have followed the German elections of November 1961, which once more returned Dr. Adenauer to power. The veteran statesman, however, decided to retire and, in 1963, was succeeded as Chancellor by Professor Dr. Ludwig Erhard. There have been the Cuban Crisis of 1962 and the deepening of the rift between China and Russia, the emergence of a strong individualistic French policy under the leadership of General de Gaulle and the hopes engendered by the Test Ban Treaty of August 5, 1963.

Yet none of these most important events in world history have directly effected the basic problems which confront Germany. The Berlin Wall and the barrier of the frontier zone still impose their shadows. There are, today, two Governments which call themselves

German. One is the Bundesrepublik, the Federal Republic of Western Germany. The other is the Deutsche Demokratische Republik, the German Democratic Republic of the Eastern Zone.

Both use the same mother tongue, both, somewhat strangely perhaps, use the same national flag, the black, red and gold of the Weimar Republic. There the resemblance ends. Although, twenty years ago they both formed part of one political whole, today there are, in east and west, different currency notes, postage stamps, police uniforms, rank insignia and army badges. In the Federal Republic of Western Germany law courts, newspapers, theatres, shops, insurance companies and steamship lines have the same outward shape and the same internal form of life as have their counterparts all over the free western world. In Eastern Germany, on the other hand all life is in increasing measure moulded to the outward show and internal meaning of the communist world which lies behind the Iron Curtain.

Of these two portions the Federal Republic is substantially the larger. In size and population it is notably similar to the United Kingdom of England and Wales, Scotland and Northern Ireland taken together. The German land surface is slightly larger than the British, ninety-five million square miles to ninety-three. The population of fifty-three million is almost exactly the same. It is a Federal Republic of eleven Länder: Baden-Württemburg, Bavaria, Berlin, Bremen, Hamburg, Hessen, North Rhine-Westphalia, Rhineland-Palatinate, Saarland, Lower Saxony and Schleswig-Holstein. The capital is at Bonn, an old university city on the Rhine. The head of the state in 1964 is President Dr. Heinrich Lübke now seventy years old. The Chancellor, who occupies a position somewhat similar to that of the British Prime Minister is Professor Dr. Ludwig Erhard, for many years Vice-Chancellor and Minister for Economics in the governments of Dr. Adenauer.

The other portion, the German Democratic Republic, the D.D.R. as it is often called, has an area a little less than half that of Western Germany and the population is only seventeen million.

The capital is at Pankow a suburb of eastern Berlin. In the days when it was the Russian Zone of an occupied Germany the area comprised the traditional divisions of Mecklenburg, Sachsen-Anhalt, Brandenburg, Saxony and Thuringia. In late years these have been abolished and replaced by fourteen new sub-divisions called Bezirke, usually bearing the name of the principal local town. The Chairman of the Council of State and the man of power in the land is Walter Ulbricht a loyal supporter of Russian policy. There are still large forces of Russian troops and airmen stationed in the D.D.R.

The story of the city of Berlin has already been told. In the western sectors there live over two million people, in the eastern sector over one million. So, in the three parts of Germany today there are: in the Federal Republic fifty-three million, in the D.D.R. seventeen million and in the whole of the city of Berlin nearly three and a half million, a grand total of well over seventy-three millions.

Where, today, in the Federal Republic there live fifty-three million there were, in 1939 only thirty nine-million. The natural increase of births over deaths accounts for part of that increase. But ten million have come into the lands of Western Germany as refugees, the "Flüchtlinge." Nearly one person out of every five inhabitants in the land today is either personally a refugee or has been born in a refugee family. It is one of the very striking achievements of the German economic recovery that this large additional population has been found employment and, to a great extent has been absorbed into the surrounding countryside. At first there was, without doubt, great hardship and distress among these newcomers and it would not be right to claim that, even now, all are free from want. Yet the achievement has been great. Western Germany which was, in any case, a highly industrialized community, has had to increase its production to give employment to the new refugee population and produce exports to pay for their food. Like Great Britain the Federal Republic must import food materials to supplement its home production and must export to pay the food bill.

In fact the industrial and commercial revival of Western Germany has been an outstanding achievement. It has been the product of hard work, sound technical ability and bold and imaginative business methods. The production of crude steel has reached the figure of thirty-three million tons and has exceeded the British output. Germany does not produce so much hard coal as Britain, 142 million tons to the British figure of 198 million, but Germany has the valuable addition of 97 million tons of brown coal or lignite burned in large local electric power stations or compressed into briquettes for domestic fuel. Moreover Germany has her own oilfields which contribute about one third of her total requirements of mineral fuel.

The overall picture is of a prosperous land, one of the great trading nations of the world, with the national currency, the Deutsche Mark, the DM of financial reports, currently regarded as one of the strongest in the world. It is proper to point out that the other Germany, the D.D.R. is not in such a strong commercial or financial position. The natural economy of the country is not so well balanced and its trading figures are not so good.

It has been shown in earlier chapters how, one thousand years ago, the boundary line between the German and the Slav tribes was not far from the present boundary between the Federal Republic and the D.D.R., the line of barbed wire and watch towers which confines the people of Mecklenburg, Sachsen-Anhalt, Thuringia and Saxony. That means that, historically regarded, Western Germany of today is the old Germany of the prince bishoprics, of the free cities, of the old university towns and of the small principalities. Most of the larger units in the history of the land, Prussia, Brandenburg and, of course, Austria, lie farther to the east. Western Germany was not a country of large landowners, nor was it "Prussian." Indeed over most of the Federal Republic, land holdings are small by English standards, perhaps too small for good

168

husbandry. Nor is it a land with a military background. Travellers used to touring the English countryside will find few memorials to past battles, few statues of famous generals. Such might have been found in old Brandenburg or Prussia but not west of the Elbe.

The federal form of constitution which has been adopted accords well with the varying historical background and the physical condition of the Länder which form the Republic. On the map the country is long and thin, from the Danish border to the Lake of Constance. There is a marked waist in the middle where Russian-occupied Thuringia makes a bulge westward. Schleswig and Holstein are agricultural countries, with fishing villages along the coast line and long standing traditions of links with Scandinavia. The two Hanseatic cities of Hamburg and Bremen are important centres of commerce and banking, busied with ships and ship-building. Both have ancient republican traditions and much sturdy independence. Most of Lower Saxony lies athwart the North German Plain. Near the coast and along the river valleys the soil is fertile and the farmers are prosperous but on the heath lands the soil is light and life is a hard struggle. Hanover and Oldenburg still cherish the memories of their old independent princely houses. Further south in Westphalia, the land is richer, as can be seen from the orchards and gardens and prosperous farmsteads. The industrial area of the Ruhr is one of the largest concentrations of mining and machinery in the world.

The Rhine Valley still carries the outward signs of its twenty centuries of civilization. Here also are French and Italian influences modifying the more typically German style found in the north and east. In Swabia and notably around Stuttgart, there is another important group of industrial centres. The Swabians have for many centuries been reputed to be thrifty cautious folk, hard and shrewd bargainers. Bavaria, in many ways the most individualistic of all the Länder, is dominated both by its mountains and by its proximity to the southern lands. Linked in the Middle Ages by river traffic with Austria and by the highway over the Brenner with Rome and with Venice, Munich has always been a point of contact with Italian thought and influence.

In these days the Flüchtlinge, spread over all the traditional cities, counties and principalities of Western Germany, have brought with them, out of the east, other traditions and memories of other ways of life. Some of these have come from Prussia, some from Silesia or Pomerania, some from the Sudeten lands. The older folk among them tend to cling together and in their Landsmannschaften, with their nostalgic reunions, they dream of the days when they shall return to their lost homelands. The younger generation have married, it may be into the local population, perhaps into other refugee families, but by very reason of the dispersion it is but seldom that husband and wife will have come from the same lost countryside. They will have established themselves, secured employment, built a house and commenced to raise a family. For these couples the picture of the ancient eastern homeland is fading.

Not all refugees have come from lands beyond the Oder-Neisse line or from the Sudeten lands. Many are from Brandenburg, Mecklenburg or Saxony, from out of the D.D.R. There are also hundreds of men of letters, artists, musicians, doctors, professors and lawyers who have come from the divided Berlin of today to seek employment in Hamburg or Dusseldorf or the other large cities of the west. These people are indeed counting the years till Berlin shall once again be the capital city of a re-united Germany.

Any generalization involves the risk of oversimplification. Yet it may be said that three main currents of thought may be identified in Western Germany as it is today. The first is a deep-rooted fear of war and all that it brings with it, coupled with the realization that any war of the future could hardly fail to be especially disastrous to a country so exposed as Western Germany. This has led to a marked reluctance to accept the need for rearmament. Then there is a strong dislike for Communism and a fear of Communistic Russia. This has led to the conviction among most that Germany's place must be with the Western world. Thirdly there is an intense desire to see the two parts of Germany re-united in an atmosphere of freedom. How all this is to be achieved is an unsolved problem.

It is nearly a score of years since the Oder-Neisse line, the Zones of Occupation, the Sectors of Berlin, came into existence as bitter realities. It would be hard to say today that they have become any less real.

On the other hand the European Community has become a working entity. The special emphasis laid on its development by General de Gaulle would not be approved by all Germans. Much has, however, been gained. There is a strong feeling that Western Europe must remain together and work together. Many would add the thought that the world has progressed to a condition where war between France and Germany or Germany and Great Britain is now unthinkable.

Federal Germany has had a parliamentary system now for some fifteen years. On the whole the system has worked well. It suits the German tradition. In the early Middle Ages democratic government on the local level was as far advanced in Germany as it was in England. Even during the depressing reaction which followed the Thirty Years War the Hanseatic cities of Lubeck, Bremen and Hamburg maintained the tradition of elected representative self government. At a time when parliamentary forms are under attack in many parts of the globe it will be to the good of Europe and the world if such institutions can become securely established in Germany. Quite certainly the fifty-three million inhabitants of the Federal Republic form a vital block of hard-working and able humanity whose influence on the future may be expected to be as important as it has been in the past. They have decided, by free vote in secret ballot, to govern themselves by parliament and to be associated with the Western world.

It must be the hope of all that the time will surely come when the other seventeen million Germans in the D.D.R. will also be able to decide their own fate, by free vote in secret ballot. Until that day arrives there must always be an unsolved question, an illness, in the very heart of Europe.

INDEX